A Firm Foundation

Building a Household of Faith on the Unchanging
Principles of the Word of God

PAUL CHAPPELL

Striving Together Publications
4020 E. Lancaster Blvd.
Lancaster, CA 93535
800.201.7748

Cover design by Daniel Irmler
Layout by Craig Parker
Edited by Robert Byers, Cary Schmidt, and Esther Brown

ISBN 978–0-9652859–6-4

Printed in the United States of America

Table of Contents

Dedication

To Terrie...thank you for twenty-five years of loving, laboring, and building on the foundational truths of God's Word. I see your godly spirit in our children and cherish the friendship and wisdom you share with me every day.

Preface

The Christian home is under attack today, as never before. Increasingly, even Christians are becoming less knowledgeable and committed to biblical truth and how it should be the guiding force in every home. More than ever, Christians are being programmed by a secular philosophy of marriage and family, and the results are devastating.

Christian marriages are falling apart in record numbers and Christian families are more confused and directionless than they have ever been. Parents are at a loss with "what to do" as they raise their children, and spouses are often throwing up their hands in futility—as if their marriages are beyond repair.

Yet, there is hope! God's Word is still true, He is still the Author and Designer of the home, and His plan still works for those who will commit themselves to it. God's promises can still be claimed, and His Word still has the answers!

Friend, your marriage and family can survive the massive assault of the enemy. You don't have to be a statistic! Your marriage is worth the spiritual fight it will take to make it strong. Your kids are worth the spiritual investment it will take to nurture them into a real relationship with God. Your family can truly become a home of Christ-like nurturing, heavenly happiness, and a shared lifetime of companionship, friendship, and worship. This is all yours, for the claiming, if you will but seek God's grace, submit to His plan, and move forward in His strength!

In a culture where the principles of the Bible are increasingly thought of as extreme or irrelevant, this book will call you back to the basics. Each chapter is filled with powerful insight, practical application, and foundational truth that will transform your home. Every page will directly challenge you to bring your family in line with God's design.

The chapters, originally derived from pulpit messages on the home, have been personally edited and revised by Dr. Chappell, carefully expanded with personal illustrations and applications, and then concluded with a memory verse and eight follow-up questions. These questions are designed not only to review the material in each chapter, but also to provoke heart-level introspection and candid discussion between you and your spouse and, perhaps, the rest of your family.

It is our prayer that you will carefully digest each chapter as a family, share the thoughts that challenge or convict you, and work through the study questions together to further grow in your family relationships.

This book would also make a great Sunday school student manual for an adult class. In the near future, a companion teacher's guide will be available for the adult teacher who would like to present these truths as a thirteen to twenty-six week Sunday school series. However God leads you to use this material, it is our sincere prayer that your own family will benefit greatly, and that you can pass along these truths to others whom you influence for God's glory!

On a personal note, I have known Dr. Paul Chappell for over twenty years and have served on his staff for much of that time.

God has given me the privilege of seeing his children grow from birth to adulthood. The things he preaches and teaches about the home are not only solidly biblical, they are actively lived out in the Chappell family. The fruit of this biblical foundation is evident in Pastor Chappell's marriage, children, and family life. Having learned from his preaching and his living example, I am eternally grateful for the profound impact that the Chappell family has had on my own family, as we strive to follow them as they follow Christ. Thank you, Pastor, for so faithfully preaching the truth, and for so effectively living and practicing it, as well!

Friend, in a world where families are falling apart in the shifting sands of cultural decline, may God use the truths of this book to place your family on the rock-solid foundation of Jesus Christ! May you truly be the wise man...for we all know where he built his house!

Sincerely,

Cary Schmidt
Associate Pastor
Lancaster Baptist Church
Striving Together Publications

PART ONE

Principles for Your Marriage

CHAPTER ONE

Faith in God's Plan for Your Marriage

And the Lord God said, It is not good that the man should be alone; I will make an help meet for him. And out of the ground the Lord God formed every beast of the field, and every fowl of the air; and brought them unto Adam to see what he would call them: and whatsoever Adam called every living creature, that was the name thereof. And Adam gave names to all cattle, and to the fowl of the air, and to every beast of the field; but for Adam there was not found an help meet for him. And the Lord God caused a deep sleep to fall upon Adam, and he slept: and he took one of his ribs, and closed up the flesh instead thereof; And the rib, which the Lord God had taken from man, made he a woman, and brought her unto the man. And Adam said, This is now bone of my bones, and flesh of my flesh: she shall be called Woman, because she was taken out of Man. Therefore shall a man leave his father and his mother, and shall cleave unto his wife: and they shall be one flesh. And they were both

naked, the man and his wife, and were not ashamed.
—Genesis 2:18–25

About one year ago, my wife Terrie and I began making plans to build a new home for our family. Although I had been involved in many large building programs, this one would be the most "personal."

Of course, the whole process for building the home began with selecting a floor plan and drawing the plans. Somewhat hurriedly, we selected our first architect. He seemed nice enough, and outwardly, everything seemed fine. Unfortunately, several months and several thousand dollars later, we learned from our builder, the truss company, and others that his blueprints were beyond deficient—they were unusable!

Quickly we realized we needed new plans! With the help of our builder and a new architect, we were able to receive our building permit; and several months later, we moved into our home.

The architect and, of course, the house plans were vital! Much more important than our residence, however, is the family we are building for God's glory. It is vital that we learn God's plan for building a Christian home!

In Genesis 2, we see principles that define God's idea of what marriage should be like. God has a plan for your marriage. He knows what will make it work to His honor and glory and to your happiness and success. You need to determine to learn and follow God's plan for your marriage in faith to reach His ultimate design.

The problem is that we live in a world which has different ideas from what God intends. Our humanistic society thinks God's plan is outdated, old-fashioned, and obsolete. As a result many people, including many Christians, have lost their faith in God's plan for marriage.

It reminds me of a story I heard about a man and his wife who decided to take a drive together. As they were driving along, the engine began to sputter, and they had to pull over to the side of the road. The man got out and opened the hood. He was angry and upset that the car was giving him mechanical problems.

It was a fairly new Ford, and he did not expect to have car trouble. Soon, a man came along and offered to help. The driver was so angry that he refused the offer. He told the man who had stopped to help, "I'm just sick of Fords." The passing motorist again offered his help and, again, it was refused. As he prepared to leave, the stranger said, "Well, I thought I'd offer my help. My name is Henry Ford."

Not accepting the help of Henry Ford was a very unwise choice by the motorist. Ford knew how the car was designed, and how every part was supposed to function. He could have easily helped the man, but the man did not want his help. Too many people today are doing the same thing to God.

God is the designer of marriage. God originated the home. He brought Eve to Adam and performed the first wedding ceremony there in the Garden of Eden. Then why is it that millions of families will go everywhere except to God for help?

Perhaps it is pride. Perhaps we are afraid the Bible will tell us to do something we do not want to do. Perhaps we are afraid that if we look to the Lord, we may have to change some things about the way we live. Whatever the reason, it is foolish to reject the counsel and advice of the One who originated the family when we need it so much.

Some of the things in this chapter are not "politically correct," but my goal is not to be politically correct. I want to be biblically correct. The things the Bible says about the home are not culturally accepted. In fact, some people think what the Bible says about how a family should be structured is weird.

Frankly, I think what the world is producing is weird. If you take a look at the average family, you are going to find things that I do not want for my family. Many of the same people who make fun of God's plan are seeing their relationships fail at record rates.

We need to go to the Bible and see what God has to say about His design and plan for the home.

If you desire your marriage to be a reflection of God's love, the world is going to think you are weird. If your desire for your children is that they would walk in obedience and respect, you are going to be out of step with the culture. If you want to raise up a generation that reflects what the Bible says, you are going to have to follow God's instructions and be willing to swim against the current.

If you put your faith in God's plan for marriage, you will never be sorry. By putting faith in God, your marriage and family will stand the test of time.

The Purpose of Marriage

God designed marriage for a reason. It has become popular today to describe marriage as an artifact of society. But marriage is part of God's divine plan and has been from the very beginning of creation. God said, *"It is not good that the man should be alone"* (Genesis 2:18). That is the first thing God said was not good. If you go back and look at Genesis chapter one, God repeatedly said that everything He made was good.

But when God looked at Adam, it was clear that Adam needed something that he did not have. There are two vital things marriage is designed to provide.

Companionship

God noticed Adam's incompleteness. God had pity on his solitude. I really believe that for most men, that is how it is—God looks at us and says, "Boy, do they need help!" When I went off to Bible college, there were many things I did not understand about life.

I thought that clean clothes magically appeared, folded in the drawers and on hangers in the closet. When I got to college, I found out there was a process that involved washing, drying, ironing, and folding. Some of the clothing I wore in college did not reflect that process.

One day I went to a laundromat. I had a suit that was dirty, so I put it in the washing machine. I put in a lot of soap and turned the water to hot so it would get good and clean. I think it was half the original size when I took it out!

There were definite needs in my life. God looked at me and said, "It is not good for him to be alone." God knows the needs of His creation. He knows that we have social appetites and a desire for companionship. Marriage according to God's design allows our need for companionship to be met.

God created Eve specifically to meet the needs Adam had. No one could possibly have done a better job designing her, because God, having created Adam, perfectly understood every need in his personality and nature. He knew how lonely Adam was, and He knew how to meet that need.

It is interesting to note that, although Adam had perfect communion and fellowship with God before sin entered into the world, there was still something missing in his life. God has designed us to need each other. Marriage is part of God's plan for meeting that need.

Proverbs 18:22 says, *"Whoso findeth a wife findeth a good thing, and obtaineth favour of the Lord."* In the Garden of Eden, God planned the institution of marriage to meet our needs for companionship.

Completion

The Bible says, *"There was not found an help meet for him"* (Genesis 2:20). The word translated "help meet" means a completer. God caused a deep sleep to fall on Adam and made Eve from one of his ribs. Eve was taken from Adam's side to be his companion.

She was not taken from Adam's head to rule over him, nor was she taken from his feet to be under him.

Everything Adam was not, Eve was. They were designed to come together and complete one another within the relationship. Society around us is intent on blurring and removing the differences between men and women. If we view them properly, we recognize that those differences are a gift from God. He has given us to each other to supply what we lack in ourselves. Men and women are very different. God designed marriage and put couples together—men and women—to supply what each is missing.

Your spouse is God's gift to you. God gave you a husband or wife to help you reach His goals for your life. Eve was designed by God specifically to complete what Adam was missing. God created Eve and presented her to Adam.

One of my favorite parts of the wedding ceremony is when the bride is brought forward by her father. I always watch the father to see how he handles it. I have two daughters, so I know my turn is coming! I ask the question, "Who giveth this woman to be married to this man?" The dad will answer, "Her mother and I." Then he places his daughter's hand on the arm of his soon-to-be son-in-law.

That is a picture of what God did in the Garden of Eden. He brought Eve to Adam and gave her to him. God's purpose for your marriage is that you and your spouse will draw close to Him and to each other, and together you might have companionship and be complete.

People have all kinds of ways of looking at the creation of woman. I heard one woman say, "God made man, looked at him, and said, 'I can do better than that.'" A man replied, "God made the world, the beasts, and man, then he rested. He made woman, and neither the world, the beasts, nor man has rested since."

There is a lot of humor on the topic of gender differences, but when we look at things from a biblical perspective, we see that both man and woman were created differently according to God's perfect design. After God created them, He brought them together to meet His divine purpose for marriage.

The Proclamation about Marriage

When God brought Eve to Adam, Adam made a statement that reveals the design and plan God had in mind for marriage. Adam said, *"This is now bone of my bones, and flesh of my flesh"* (Genesis 2:23). He totally embraced and accepted the gift God had brought to him.

A Proclamation of Acceptance

Adam was overwhelmed with the goodness of God in creating Eve for him. Imagine what it must have been like for Adam to have all of creation brought before him, only to realize that in all the world there was no one else like him. He was facing a lonely existence.

Husbands, let me speak to you for a moment. One of the most important foundations of marriage is acceptance. At the beginning of your relationship, there was acceptance. During courtship, men are attuned to the good characteristics of the woman they love. The problem is that, over time, you can become more attuned to the negative than the positive.

Sometimes when I am counseling a couple, the man will say, "Yeah, I loved her once, but I was young and stupid back then." I tell him, "You're still stupid; you've just gotten older." The fact is that there was a time in your life when you fell in love, and nothing she did seemed to be wrong. You were in an accepting mode.

By the way, men, you were seeking the same thing. You were looking for someone to accept and love you. You found it in her. Acceptance builds the early relationship. The lack of acceptance that can develop over time destroys relationships.

When you begin to criticize, critique, and judge your spouse, the foundation of the relationship begins to crumble. As we become accustomed to living with a person, we can lose sight of his or her good qualities and begin to focus on little annoyances. If you allow that spirit in your heart, you are undermining your relationship. You must recognize the importance of acceptance in your marriage.

Vietnam veteran Dave Reaver was in the field fighting against the Viet Cong. He pulled the pin on a phosphorus grenade, and it malfunctioned. His face and hands were covered with the burning phosphorus. To try to gain relief, he ran into a nearby pond of water, but the water only spread the flames across his body. His face began to crack from the intense heat as it burned.

Dave was a committed Christian, and his squad mates heard him yell, "God, I still love you!" as agony racked his body. Finally, the medics were able to put out the fire, and he was evacuated from the country for treatment. When he saw himself in a mirror for the first time, he found his face to be horribly disfigured.

In his autobiography, he tells about wondering what his wife Nancy would think. He wondered if she would be willing to be seen with him. There was a man in the bed next to him who was a double amputee. He had lost both of his legs in the war. That man's wife came to see him three times. On the third visit, she took off her wedding ring and laid it on his bed. She said, "I'm sorry. I married a man, not a cripple. I can't stay with you."

A few days later, Dave woke up to find Nancy standing beside his bed. She knelt down and kissed him and said, "Welcome home, Dave. I love you, and I'm glad you're here." She was giving him the gift every marriage needs on a regular basis—the gift of unconditional acceptance. Every wife needs that acceptance. Every husband needs that acceptance.

From the very beginning, God's design for marriage was that it would provide acceptance. Adam had been working out in the animal kingdom and realized there was no match for him there. Eve immediately caught his attention. She was not a process of evolution; she was a designed creation of God. He expressed his acceptance.

Instead of looking at faults, focus on the blessings. One of the best ways to keep a spirit of acceptance is to daily thank God for what He has given you in your spouse. Rather than grumbling and complaining about what you think is missing, express gratitude for what you have. Remember, your spouse is God's gift to you.

A Proclamation of Honor

First Peter 3:7 says, *"Likewise, ye husbands, dwell with them according to knowledge, giving honour unto the wife, as unto the weaker vessel, and as being heirs together of the grace of life; that your prayers be not hindered."*

God not only proclaims the necessity of acceptance in marriage, but He also commands a husband to honor his wife.

The first thing we need to determine is what God means when He refers to a woman as the "weaker vessel." Many people react negatively to that because they do not understand what it means. In no way is God saying that women are inferior to men.

Remember, God specifically designed women. Eve was unique among God's creation. God gives great honor to women, and He commands their husbands to do so as well. Referring to the wife as the "weaker vessel" is simply an acknowledgement of the physical differences between men and women.

God created men and women differently according to His design. So we see then a need for marriage to be a place of honor. Although this command in 1 Peter is specifically addressed to husbands, I believe honor needs to flow both directions in the marriage relationship.

Husbands need to demonstrate honor to their wives. It is a great joy for a Christian husband to hold a door open for his wife, to express his appreciation for her, to lift something for her, or to comfort her when she's struggling with something emotionally. She needs to know she is special to him.

Wives need to demonstrate honor to their husbands. Far too often cruel and cutting words are spoken in public. The virtuous woman has the "law of kindness" in her words (Proverbs 31:26). Men need to know that they are appreciated. They need to hear expressions of honor from their wives.

Honor is based on an appreciation for what God did in bringing us together as partners in marriage. Adam recognized immediately that Eve was not just another animal. I believe when he saw her he said something like, "Wow! You're the most beautiful thing I've ever seen. Thank you, God!"

Adam realized Eve was something special. Your spouse is God's gift to you. He or she deserves to be honored and recognized as such. Your desire should be to be a blessing to your spouse. You should want your spouse to know how you feel about him or her, and you need to express your feelings audibly. That kind of honor builds a strong marriage.

The Priorities of Marriage

For your marriage to be what God wants it to be, it has to have the place of importance that He planned for it to hold in your life. Some things have to be most important. If your marriage is to reach God's highest goal, three convictions must remain priority items.

Leaving

At the very first wedding, Adam said, "Therefore shall a man leave his father and his mother." That is a surprising statement if you stop to think about it. He didn't have parents to leave, but he was expressing a principle that would apply to all the marriages that would follow his.

There must be a separation for your marriage to succeed. Leaving means that we must abandon one relationship before establishing the next relationship. There has to be a break from the past. You have to leave behind, completely sever, any old relationships or emotional attachments.

Many marriages are destroyed because one spouse still has unresolved feelings for someone else. The marriage vows say, "forsaking all others," and that needs to be the way you enter into marriage. There must be a leaving of romantic attachment from anyone else other than your spouse.

There also needs to be a physical and emotional leaving of the extended families. Though young married couples should honor their parents, seek their counsel, and express love and appreciation, they must also learn to build their *own* families and make their *own* decisions.

Sometimes parents are very controlling. They try to use guilt to manipulate the young couple into doing things the way they want them done. They want to be involved in decisions that are not theirs to make. The new couple must draw lines and boundaries to recognize they are their own family unit, and God places the primary responsibility on the husband.

Be careful not to create a breach in the relationship with your parents, but for your marriage to succeed, a psychological and physical leaving of parents is needed to establish your own relationship.

Cleaving

Adam also said a man should "cleave unto his wife." Some of you reading this have already been through a divorce. I understand the statistics and their implications, but we need to realize that God's plan is for marriages to stay together.

So often I hear people use the excuse that things are going rough. "It's just hard. She's not attractive anymore. He's just so lazy." God's desire and purpose for your marriage is that you will seek His grace to overcome the obstacles and problems and stay together.

The word *cleave* means to be glued together. Maybe you are old enough to remember the Super Glue commercial where the construction worker dangled from his hard hat, glued to a steel beam several stories high. The advertisers were trying to demonstrate a bond that could not be broken. That is what marriage is supposed to be.

Jesus taught on the permanence of marriage in the New Testament. He saw that husbands and wives were not staying together. Jesus said that was not God's plan.

"For this cause shall a man leave his father and mother, and cleave to his wife; And they twain shall be one flesh: so then they are no more twain, but one flesh. What therefore God hath joined together, let not man put asunder" (Mark 10:7–9).

You need to eliminate the concept of divorce from your thinking and vocabulary. My wife Terrie and I made some ground rules when we began our marriage nearly twenty-five years ago. One of the things we promised each other was that we would never even talk about the possibility of getting a divorce, no matter what happened.

So many couples threaten to call an attorney every time things get tough. Do not resort to that. God's plan is for you to "stick like glue" to your spouse. I am opposed to pre-nuptial agreements. I do not think you should ever make a provision for your marriage to fail. Instead, you should dedicate yourself to doing whatever it takes to keep it together.

This is the commitment that we make in our wedding vows: "For better for worse; for richer for poorer; in sickness and in health." What you promised God and your spouse was that you would stay together no matter what happened. You need to commit to living up to that vow.

Winston Churchill once said, "Wars are not won by evacuations." Too many couples are giving up on their marriages rather than doing all they can to stick together. That is why the divorce rate is so high—men and women are not committed to cleaving to each other.

Weaving

Marriage is two people becoming "one flesh." That is God's design. Yet so many couples start out on the wrong foot. They keep separate bank accounts. They plan to go on separate vacations so they can keep their own space. They each have their own friends and do not spend time together.

What they are entering into is more of a partnership than a weaving of a close relationship. Too many couples are more like roommates than husband and wife. That is not God's plan for marriage. God's plan is for your marriage relationship to be deeply intimate on every level.

Terrie and I have found that for us to "weave together" in an intimate and close heart relationship, we must carve out spiritual time together. Besides daily talks or eating out together at a restaurant, we have created special days, four or five times a year on our calendar, where we can get away for a day trip or even overnight together just to talk about our marriage, children, schedule, and future.

WEAVING SPIRITUALLY

The best advice I can give you for spiritual growth is to read the Bible together. Read the same Scripture passage separately and then talk about what you learned from it. Set aside times to pray together. Go to a solid, Bible-preaching and teaching church together.

Build each other's relationship with God. Do not ever discourage a spiritual interest that is shown by your spouse. If your spouse wants to do something that will draw him or her closer to God, encourage it.

Terrie and I try to read a new book on marriage at least twice a year. We then sit down and talk about what we have learned. This helps us to grow closer as we look for ways to strengthen our relationship. Each of us must work at developing the spiritual part of our marriage.

One of the great secrets to success in reaching God's plan for your marriage is building on a spiritual foundation. The truth is that when you both draw closer to God, you are automatically drawn closer to each other at the same time. Invest in the spiritual aspect of your marriage.

WEAVING EMOTIONALLY

We cannot have the kind of relationship God wants unless we spend time together. One of the great dangers to marriage is allowing our time to be scattered. Your spouse needs to know that he or she is important enough to you to deserve the investment of your time.

There are so many good opportunities that can easily distract us from the priority of building our marriages on an emotional plane. Your marriage must matter more to you than a promotion at work, a night out with your friends, or a hobby. I encourage people to be actively involved in the work and ministries of their churches. Yet sometimes people can become so involved in serving that they forget the main thing.

When Jesus visited the house of Mary and Martha, Martha was very busy trying to get the meal to be perfect. She was frustrated that Mary was sitting at Jesus' feet instead of helping her. Jesus told Martha that, though she was doing good things, she was missing the most important thing (Luke 10:38–42).

I know pastors who have lost their wives and children, because they focused solely on the church and ignored the needs at home. God wants your closest emotional relationship to be with your spouse. Nothing should be allowed to come between you.

On a very practical level, you and your spouse need to be recreational partners who do things together. Find things that you enjoy doing with each other. Go for walks or on dates. Cultivate your time together. Make an investment of time in building emotional intimacy in your marriage.

WEAVING PHYSICALLY

"Now concerning the things whereof ye wrote unto me: It is good for a man not to touch a woman. Nevertheless, to avoid fornication, let every man have his own wife, and let every woman have her own husband. Let the husband render unto the wife due benevolence: and likewise also the wife unto the husband. The wife hath not power of her own body, but the husband: and likewise also the husband hath not power of his own body, but the wife" (1 Corinthians 7:1–4).

God's plan for the physical aspect of marriage has been distorted by the Devil. We live in a sex-crazed culture. God planned physical intimacy to be a wholesome, unifying force within a marriage relationship. The focus on sex in our world is destroying relationships, as people selfishly seek to satisfy their physical desires outside of God's plan.

So often sex becomes a battlefield within marriage. We need to realize that the same God who designed marriage also designed physical intimacy. It is a vital part of building the relationship. God's plan is for a husband and wife to mutually submit their bodies to each other to meet the other's needs.

One of the most destructive things you can do to your marriage is to use the physical relationship as a weapon against your spouse. Commit yourself to building a close and satisfying physical relationship.

You cannot start or build a solid relationship on just a physical basis. This is just one of the pillars of a healthy marriage. Too many Christian couples have allowed society's focus on sex to lead them to believe that it is all that matters. It is simply part of God's plan to draw you and your spouse closer together.

Marriage is designed to draw us closer together and closer to God. If you follow His plan, your marriage will succeed in fulfilling the purposes He had in mind when He brought the first couple together in the Garden of Eden. Your marriage can be happy, fulfilling, and strong as you live by faith in God's design.

Back when our home was in the "design" phase, we tried and tried to "picture" what it would look like. Sometimes Christians look at the Bible and listen to preaching, and wonder—"What will it look like? How will it turn out?" Well, Terrie and I are thankful that our home turned out better than we imagined. But more importantly, we have found that God's plan for our family has been much more than we could have imagined. I want to encourage you to let the biblical principles in this book form your blueprint for a strong family.

Study Questions

1. Why do many families turn everywhere but to God for advice about marriage?

2. What two vital things is marriage designed to provide?

3. List three convictions that must remain priorities in your marriage.

4. What is one of the most important foundations of marriage?

5. Why should you have faith in God's plan for your marriage?

6. How has your acceptance of your spouse changed since you were first married? What adjustments should be made?

7. What are some ways you can outwardly honor each other?

8. List some suggestions for growing together spiritually, emotionally, and physically. What can you do today to start applying these things?

Memory Verse

Mark 10:7–9—*"For this cause shall a man leave his father and mother, and cleave to his wife; And they twain shall be one flesh: so then they are no more twain, but one flesh. What therefore God hath joined together, let not man put asunder."*

CHAPTER TWO

Developing Oneness in Your Marriage

> *And the Lord God caused a deep sleep to fall upon Adam, and he slept: and he took one of his ribs, and closed up the flesh instead thereof; And the rib, which the Lord God had taken from man, made he a woman, and brought her unto the man. And Adam said, This is now bone of my bones, and flesh of my flesh: she shall be called Woman, because she was taken out of Man. Therefore shall a man leave his father and his mother, and shall cleave unto his wife: and they shall be one flesh. And they were both naked, the man and his wife, and were not ashamed.*—Genesis 2:21–25

I believe that there is nowhere today where a revival of unity is more needed than in the Christian family. It seems like real oneness and unity is an elusive goal for many people. Even committed Christians struggle with true intimacy in marriage.

The world expects marriage to be a scene of conflict. Dwight Eisenhower said, "Only two things are necessary to keep one's wife happy. The first is to let her think she's having her own way. The second is to let her have it." I heard about one lady who told a

21

friend, "When I married Mr. Right, I didn't know his first name was Always!"

Society accepts that there should be tension and disharmony in marriage. Today we find that many Christians settle for an uneasy truce, but that is not God's plan. He wants your marriage to be a place of blessing and harmony. You can find unity by following the plan of the Word of God for your marriage.

God created us with a need for relationships. Before the fall of creation, the world was perfect. Adam had a beautiful place in which to live. He had unhindered communion with God. Yet even in that setting, he needed a companion.

God recognized that it was "not good that the man should be alone." He created Eve so that man and woman would have companionship and unity in their relationship. It is part of His design that marriage would be a place of oneness in which to fill the needs He knows we have.

Marital oneness was attacked when sin entered into the world. It is important for you to realize that the Devil will attack your marriage. He has been doing that since the very first home in the Garden of Eden. Sin not only broke the perfect fellowship between man and God; it attacked the oneness of the marriage relationship.

If you allow sin into your home in any form—pride, lust, selfishness—it will undermine the unity and closeness of your relationship. Adam and Eve were cast out of the Garden of Eden because of their sin.

"Therefore the Lord God sent him forth from the garden of Eden, to till the ground from whence he was taken. So he drove out the man; and he placed at the east of the garden of Eden Cherubims, and a flaming sword which turned every way, to keep the way of the tree of life" (Genesis 3:23–24).

Sin is always a destructive force. The perfect world God created was lost because of sin. Death entered the world. Sickness and pain entered the world. Physical toil entered the world. Pain in childbirth entered the world. A breakdown of the oneness that God intended for marriage entered the world.

Every marriage and family will go through seasons when the unity of the home is disrupted. We can never recover the perfection of God's original creation on this earth, but we can follow His plan to build and strengthen the union and harmony in our homes.

Even in this wicked world, you can have the oneness in your marriage that God desires. That intimate relationship with your spouse is achieved by following God's design for your relationship.

A Commitment to Permanence

Too many people today enter into marriage with the idea that there is a back door. If things do not work out the way they want or expect, they can always get a divorce. It is a tragedy that our society has accepted disposable marriages. A close marriage can only develop in an atmosphere of trust and permanence.

Many people reading this are on their second marriages. Maybe you were abandoned by your spouse. If you have seen a relationship fail, your new marriage can still succeed. You need to take these same principles and apply them to your current relationship. Even if you have lived through heartbreak once, you need to be completely committed to permanence in your new marriage. Do not live with the expectation that your marriage will fail. Commit to its success.

Through Complete Acceptance

"And Adam said, This is now bone of my bones, and flesh of my flesh: she shall be called Woman, because she was taken out of Man" (Genesis 2:23).

In chapter one we talked about the need for acceptance, but I want to highlight what acceptance does to build intimacy in a relationship. The Bible teaches us that accepting our spouse is the foundation of a lasting, intimate relationship.

"So ought men to love their wives as their own bodies. He that loveth his wife loveth himself. For no man ever yet hated his own flesh; but nourisheth and cherisheth it, even as the Lord the church" (Ephesians 5:28–29).

Acceptance is the optimum environment for change. If I could convince couples of anything that would improve their relationships, it would be this fact. You cannot condition your acceptance on your spouse's reaching some level of performance. You must accept your spouse where he or she is. That is the way God treats us.

The church is called the bride of Christ. We have flaws and imperfections. Though we are an imperfect bride, Jesus loves and accepts us the way we are. Your spouse needs that kind of acceptance. Having Christ-like love means that we accept based on love, not on performance.

One of the most damaging feelings your spouse can have is that he or she is constantly on trial. You need to let your spouse know he or she is completely accepted and that you are committed to the relationship no matter what happens.

Through Complete Commitment
"Therefore shall a man leave his father and his mother, and shall cleave unto his wife: and they shall be one flesh" (Genesis 2:24).

The word that is translated *cleave* means "to glue on; to join one's self closely to; or to stick together." We also talked about cleaving in the first chapter, but it is impossible to overemphasize permanence as a key to developing an intimate relationship.

If you have ever done any kind of home improvement project, you have probably used plywood. Plywood is simply thin individual sheets of wood that are glued together in layers. Pressure is then applied as the glue dries to ensure that the wood will not come apart. That is what the word *cleave* means.

God wants your marriage to be completely committed to permanence. We do a lot of premarital counseling at our church. We try to help both the man and woman to recognize that the commitment they are making is a life-long commitment.

We still use the old fashioned wedding vows—"Till death do us part." I know of churches that have watered down their commitment to marriage. They are rewriting the vows to accommodate the times. That is not how God designed marriage. You are never going to have true oneness and intimacy if you are constantly thinking there might be a way out. To cleave is to make an unbreakable commitment.

MAKE A COMMITMENT TO PURPOSEFUL LIVING

When you get married, you have a new purpose—a cause for which you are living. You are no longer on your own. That new cause is the development of a godly family that will bring honor and glory to God.

In Mark 10:7, Jesus said, *"For this cause shall a man leave his father and mother, and cleave to his wife."* Every one of us needs to recognize that his marriage is a cause. We need to live on purpose rather than living a reactionary life. Reactionary people bounce from problem to problem rather than doing things intentionally.

You should have specific goals for the growth of your marriage. On purpose you should set out to take actions that will strengthen your relationship. I encourage you to make a written list of things you can do in the next week, the month, and year that will demonstrate your commitment to your spouse.

Set out to reach the goal of intimacy together. There is an old saying that says, "He who aims at nothing, hits it every time." Recognize, daily, that your actions and words are strengthening or weakening the oneness of your marriage.

MAKE A COMMITMENT TO BIBLICAL PRINCIPLES

Your commitment is not just to the person you married. It is also a commitment of obedience to God's plan. Before the priority of being a husband or a wife, you are a Christian. You must follow the Word of God in your daily life.

If we take care to ensure that our vertical relationship is right, our horizontal relationship will be right, as well. The best way to be a good husband is to be a good Christian. The best way to be a good wife is to be a good Christian. Dedicate your life to obeying the commands of Scripture. *"And they twain shall be one flesh: so then they are no more twain but one flesh. What therefore God hath joined together, let not man put asunder"* (Mark 10:8–9).

Do not let the world's values influence your relationship away from the Scriptures. Someone said, "A man who wants something will find a way; a man who doesn't will find an excuse." Make the commitment that you will live by Bible principles, and do not let anything pull you away from it.

You should have an understanding with your spouse that you are both going to follow what the Word of God says. There should be some things you will never do—some things that are off limits, because they are forbidden by the Bible.

Never fantasize outside the revealed will of God. God's plan is for your needs to be met within your marriage, and for your marriage to be permanent. I have counseled couples whose marriages were destroyed because one of them, even though he or she knew what God's Word said, had fantasized about finding something better outside of his or her relationship.

This kind of thinking cripples our ability to clearly discern the will of God. A husband or wife who fantasizes outside of his or her marriage cannot be a good spouse. Dream of making your marriage better. It is never God's plan for your marriage to come apart.

There will be peaks and valleys in your relationship. There will be good days and bad days. That is why you have to go into marriage with a commitment to permanence. You and your spouse must have the attitude that, no matter what happens, you will stick together.

A Commitment to Spiritual Unity

"Therefore shall a man leave his father and his mother, and shall cleave unto his wife: and they shall be one flesh" (Genesis 2:24).

I have seen couples try all sorts of things to build their relationships. I know husbands and wives who are in motorcycle clubs, sailing clubs, bowling leagues, and political committees. It is good to do things together and have common interests, but those cannot be the sole focus of your unity.

You need to have more than a few toys in common. There must be a spiritual dimension that acts as the glue that is holding your relationship together. You must work together to build spiritual unity.

Becoming "one flesh" is more than just the physical relationship in marriage. That is only part of the unity God intends for your marriage. God wants your union to be so strong and indivisible that the two of you become like one person. This can only happen as you develop your oneness on a spiritual level.

Our Highest Example of Unity

The Trinity is the greatest example of unity that we have in Scripture. The Father, the Son, and the Holy Spirit have unity in their relationship, and their unity sets a pattern we can follow in our marriages.

THE FATHER EXALTS THE SON

"God, who at sundry times and in divers manners spake in time past unto the fathers by the prophets, Hath in these last days spoken unto us by his Son, whom he hath appointed heir of all things, by whom

also he made the worlds; But unto the Son he saith, Thy throne, O God, is for ever and ever: a sceptre of righteousness is the sceptre of thy kingdom" (Hebrews 1:1–2, 8).

God the Father, speaking to the Son, said, *"Thy throne, O God."* The Father is ascribing to Jesus all the attributes and aspects of divinity. He lifts Jesus up and gives Him the praise and glory which are His due.

THE SON EXALTS THE FATHER

"Jesus saith unto them, My meat is to do the will of him that sent me, and to finish his work" (John 4:34).

"I have glorified thee on the earth: I have finished the work which thou gavest me to do" (John 17:4).

Jesus centered His life on doing things that would bring honor and glory to the Father. There is no jealousy or division between the members of the Godhead. They operate in harmony, lifting each other up and giving each other glory.

THE SPIRIT EXALTS THE SON

"Howbeit when he, the Spirit of truth, is come, he will guide you into all truth: for he shall not speak of himself; but whatsoever he shall hear, that shall he speak: and he will shew you things to come. He shall glorify me: for he shall receive of mine, and shall shew it unto you" (John 16:13–14).

All of the members of the Trinity work together to bring about our salvation. There is no spirit of selfishness or jealousy at work in their relationship. They serve as an example of what a relationship of oneness can truly be.

Our Highest Hope for Unity

I have had people say to me, "Pastor Chappell, if you knew what is going on in our marriage, you would know there is little hope for unity." With God there is always hope. He is greater than any marriage difficulty you face. Our hope for unity rests on the presence of two crucial elements.

YOU MUST KNOW CHRIST AS SAVIOUR

Both spouses need to be saved for there to be a hope for spiritual unity. There must be a time in your life when you asked Jesus to be your Saviour and accepted His payment for your sins. There is no hope of having an intimate oneness with your spouse if you are not both believers.

You cannot expect to have spiritual unity between a lost person and a saved person, or between two lost persons. That is like expecting a living person and a dead person or two dead people to carry on a conversation. It's impossible! Unity begins on the spiritual level, and both spouses must have the Holy Spirit present and working in their lives.

YOU MUST ACKNOWLEDGE CHRIST AS LORD

To have unity, you must also live in a way that reflects the control and direction of Christ as the head of your home. In John 13:13 Jesus said, *"Ye call me Master and Lord: and ye say well; for so I am."*

God places the responsibility for the leadership of the home on the husband, but the husband is not the ruler of the home—Jesus must be the King. You cannot expect to develop intimacy apart from a commitment of obedience to God. When you acknowledge Jesus as Lord, you can then begin to serve one another in love.

Unity, love, and intimacy are built when you live every day with Jesus as Lord of your life. Allow Him to guide and control your words and actions. The impact on your marriage will be powerful.

A Commitment to Openness

"And they were both naked, the man and his wife, and were not ashamed" (Genesis 2:25).

Intimacy and oneness in marriage cannot exist without openness. The nakedness of Adam and Eve is symbolic of the openness of their relationship. They had nothing to be ashamed of or to feel guilty about. They were perfectly innocent. They belonged to each other and to God.

That is how God designed marriage to be. There is to be a commitment to openness with one another. Most couples start their relationship that way. They are in love, open, and trust each other. Over time, disappointments and hurt may come and cause a closing of hearts one toward another. That closure affects your conversation, intimacy, ability to laugh, and your friendship. God did not create marriage for closed fists; He created it for open hands. To have a developing relationship, you must be willing to open yourself to your spouse.

Hindrances to Openness

The Devil knows that if he can destroy openness, he can destroy your intimacy. There are many tools in his arsenal that will impact the closeness of your relationship. Maybe some of the following have attacked your home:

SELFISHNESS

Selfishness is a desire to have your own way. It is part of our fallen nature, and it attacks openness in your marriage. Philippians 2:3 says, *"Let nothing be done through strife or vainglory; but in lowliness of mind let each esteem other better than themselves."* Put your partner's interests and desires ahead of your own.

Sometimes spouses have a picture in their minds of how they want their homes and marriages to look, and they are going to insist on having things their way. That is a recipe for a closed heart. If you are living selfishly, you cannot expect to develop a close and intimate relationship.

INSECURITY

Because of failures or problems from the past, many people live with the constant fear that something is going to go wrong in their marriages. Often this insecurity may be based on seeing divorce in their own families. This creates the feeling that they must protect themselves. Openness cannot be achieved without a willingness to be hurt. If you ever desire closeness, you must first become vulnerable. I remind you that God has not given us a spirit of fear but of power (2 Timothy 1:7). He can conquer your feelings of insecurity.

COMPETITION

God did not create a husband and wife to be in competition; He created them for completion. Sometimes a spirit of competition is very subtle and slow to be revealed. It is often seen in families in which both spouses work. Statistics tell us that women make up forty-seven percent of the workforce.[1]

"Put on therefore, as the elect of God, holy and beloved, bowels of mercies, kindness, humbleness of mind, meekness, longsuffering" (Colossians 3:12).

We had a couple in our church, years ago, who could have fallen prey to competition. They both worked, and then the husband lost his job. The wife kept a humble spirit through the process. She did not blame her husband for the job loss. She did not accuse him of failing to provide.

She never said, "I'm making the money now, so I should make the decisions." She followed his leadership even though he was unemployed. Soon he was back to work and things returned to normal. It was her spirit that kept their marriage from declining into a competitive relationship.

---

[1] Women Employed Institute survey of economic data published April 2004 on their website, www.womenemployed.org

UNMET NEEDS AND EXPECTATIONS

An expectation is an unwritten contract. It is something that is written in your heart. Young husbands often expect to walk in from work and smell roast beef, mashed potatoes, and gravy. Young wives expect their husbands to come home from work and talk for an hour about the day.

Most people enter marriage with at least a few unrealistic and unspoken expectations. When those ideals are not met, disappointment can close the heart. The Bible solution to unmet needs is understanding.

"Likewise, ye husbands, dwell with them according to knowledge, giving honour unto the wife, as unto the weaker vessel, and as being heirs together of the grace of life; that your prayers be not hindered" (1 Peter 3:7).

You need to understand your spouse's needs and wants. Take time to discover the wants, and do your best to make the dreams come true. At the same time, it is important not to be a slave to your unrealistic expectations. Realize that your spouse is a human being with weaknesses and idiosyncrasies of his own.

A couple brought their first baby home from the hospital. The wife suggested to her husband that he try his hand at changing diapers. He said, "I'm busy right now. I'll change the next one." The next time the baby was wet, the wife asked her husband if he was ready to learn how to change diapers. He looked at her with a somewhat puzzled look and then said, "I didn't mean the next diaper, Honey. I meant the next baby!" Obviously this husband has a lot to learn. Yours may have much to learn as well, but growth is always possible by the grace of God.

Helps to Openness

Here are three specific tools that will help you open up to your spouse and encourage him to open up to you. You need to seek God's grace to make sure that these attitudes are a part of your relationship.

ACCEPTING

To accept your spouse is to be content with your spouse. You have the choice to try to change your spouse to make him or her what you want him or her to be, or you can choose to realize that God has given your spouse to you as a gift to complete your life.

"Let your conversation be without covetousness; and be content with such things as ye have: for he hath said, I will never leave thee, nor forsake thee" (Hebrews 13:5).

Comparison to others is dangerous. I hear this often when counseling couples: "Her husband does this. His wife does that." Comparison breeds discontent. We have to guard our hearts against the "grass is greener" syndrome. The grass is not really greener. Even if it were, you would still have to mow it. Your grass will green up if you fertilize, water, and care for it. God accepts us, and we are to accept each other.

YIELDING

We must be willing to yield to each other. A spirit of oneness is only created as we surrender our opinions and desires to each other. This will not happen unless we learn to yield to the Holy Spirit within. Yielding to Him helps you yield to your spouse.

"Submitting yourselves one to another in the fear of God" (Ephesians 5:21).

Do not insist on having everything your way. Focus on serving your spouse. Do not measure the success of your relationship by what you are getting. Measure it by what you give. Be patient.

It is important that you understand that I am not talking about giving in to sin or wrongdoing. God's plan for yieldedness is that you surrender your preferences to honor your partner. Rather than fighting for your way, submit yourself to meeting the dreams of your spouse. If both of you are yielding, you will find it easy to open your hearts to each other.

APPRECIATING

Express your appreciation for your spouse on a regular basis. Let him or her know what you appreciate. There is something in our nature that thrives on receiving expressions of appreciation. Mark Twain said, "I can live for a month on a good compliment."

"A wholesome tongue is a tree of life: but perverseness therein is a breach in the spirit" (Proverbs 15:4).

Maybe you are like me. I can walk into a room, and the first ten things I see are things that need to get fixed. If you are like that, you have to be extra careful not to express criticism all the time. Look for the things that are right. Find positive aspects you can praise.

The Bible tells us that good words bring life and beauty to a relationship (Proverbs 25:11). If we will learn how to appreciate the small victories and express that appreciation, other victories will follow. Express love and appreciation. Remember that it is hard to live with a critical person. Do not be one. Express your gratitude and appreciation regularly to your spouse.

Is your relationship open, or has it started to close down? God can restore your marriage. His plan is that you commit to permanence, unity, and openness. As you do, the oneness in your marriage will grow and deepen. You can have a happy marriage! Do not settle for anything less than God's design!

Study Questions

1. To develop oneness in marriage, what three commitments should you make to/with your spouse?

2. What two things are essential for permanence in marriage?

3. What is the best way to be a good husband/wife?

4. The Devil knows that if he can destroy openness, he can destroy your intimacy. What four things does he use to hinder openness in a relationship?

5. List some things you can do in the next week, month, and year that will demonstrate your commitment to your spouse.

6. Compare and contrast the relationship between you and your spouse to the relationship of the Trinity.

7. How can you fight the Devil's attacks on openness in your marriage?

8. Accepting, yielding to, and appreciating your spouse encourages openness in your relationship. In which attitude(s) do you need to grow the most? What will you do to see growth?

Memory Verse

Ephesians 5:28–29—*"So ought men to love their wives as their own bodies. He that loveth his wife loveth himself. For no man ever yet hated his own flesh; but nourisheth and cherisheth it, even as the Lord the church:"*

CHAPTER THREE

How to Have a Truly Christian Home

*And the Lord God said, It is not good that the man
should be alone: I will make him an help meet for him.
And the Lord God caused a deep sleep to fall upon
Adam and he slept: and he took one of his ribs, and
closed up the flesh instead thereof; And the rib, which
the Lord God had taken from man, made he a woman,
and brought her unto the man. And Adam said, This
is now bone of my bones, and flesh of my flesh: she
shall be called Woman, because she was taken out of
Man. Therefore shall a man leave his father and his
mother, and shall cleave unto his wife: and they shall
be one flesh.*—Genesis 2:18, 21–24

From the very beginning of humanity, the family has been the basic
building block of society. God instituted the family as part of His
plan for the people He had created. God planned for the Christian
home according to His knowledge of His creation.

The home is to be a place where God's love is modeled and
the next generation is mentored in their faith. The only way to
have a truly Christian home is to follow the guidelines of God's

Word. Many people do not understand what a Christian home is. Some think that, because they live in America, they are somehow automatically Christians. That is not true.

Being an American or going to a church does not make you a Christian. You must make the decision to become a Christian. If you are a believer, that does not mean that you automatically have a Christian home. Let's look, then, at the requirements, according to God's Word, for having a truly Christian home.

Salvation through Jesus Christ

Before your home can truly be labeled as a Christian home, the members of the family who are of age must be saved. Salvation is the fundamental building block of a Christian home.

Parents Must Teach the Doctrines of Christ

It is your responsibility, as parents, to teach your children about salvation. Paul recounted this process in 2 Timothy 1:5 when he said, *"When I call to remembrance the unfeigned faith that is in thee, which dwelt first in thy grandmother Lois, and thy mother Eunice; and I am persuaded that in thee also."*

Timothy had teachers, in his mother and grandmother, who explained and lived a personal faith in Jesus Christ. It is important to remember that having saved parents does not save the child. Each child needs to learn what the Bible teaches about sin and his individual responsibility to accept Christ as Saviour.

We need to give our children a heritage of faith. We need to pass on to them what we have learned of the things of God. A parent's first and most important job is to teach his children how to be saved.

The very first week I came to pastor the church in Lancaster, I went out and knocked on several hundred doors, witnessing and inviting people to church. It was a tumultuous time in our lives. We were trying to learn where everything was in a new city. There were boxes everywhere in our little apartment.

On the Saturday night before our first service, I came home to the apartment we had rented. The cooler was broken, and it was hot. I was a little discouraged. But the first thing my wife said to me when I walked in the door was, "You need to talk to Danielle. She wants to get saved."

Immediately, I forgot all about the doors that had been shut in my face. I forgot all the people who said they were not interested in the church. I forgot the heat, the broken cooler, and the boxes. My oldest child wanted to trust Christ! What a blessing that my own daughter was the first convert baptized in our church.

We cannot neglect to teach salvation to our children. You will never know a better day as a parent than the day your last child accepts Christ as Saviour and you know that your family will never be eternally divided. Prepare your children's hearts so they will be open to the conviction and prompting of the Holy Spirit.

Salvation Is a Personal Choice

We cannot "get saved" *for* our children. We can lead the way, and teach them the truth. Every child must accept Christ for himself. In 2 Timothy 3:15, Paul said, *"And that from a child thou hast known the holy scriptures, which are able to make thee wise unto salvation through faith which is in Christ Jesus."*

Timothy made a spiritual decision based on the training he received from his mother and grandmother. But it ultimately had to be his own decision. The responsibility of parents is to carefully point the way to Jesus. We need to be careful not to give our children a false hope of salvation. Every child must learn that salvation is a personal choice he must make himself.

In Romans 10:17, the Bible says, *"So then faith cometh by hearing, and hearing by the word of God."* Our part is to ensure that our children hear and learn the Bible so that the Holy Spirit can touch their hearts. Nothing is more important than to teach our children the Scriptures.

Surrender to the Holy Spirit

The second important requirement of a truly Christian home is that the members have surrendered their will to the Holy Spirit. A person who is not a believer cannot surrender to the Holy Spirit, because the Spirit is not a part of his life.

"So then they that are in the flesh cannot please God. But ye are not in the flesh, but in the Spirit, if so be that the Spirit of God dwell in you. Now if any man have not the Spirit of Christ, he is none of his" (Romans 8:8–9).

Those of us who are saved have the Holy Spirit of God dwelling within us. Yet it is possible for us to have the Spirit but not be following His leading and direction. Picture two glasses of water and two packets of Alka-Seltzer. If you open one of the packets and drop the tablets into the water, there is an immediate reaction. You can quickly tell that the "plop-plop, fizz-fizz" has started.

If you drop the other tablets into the water without opening the packet, there will be no reaction. The water and the power of the medicine are the same, but it has not been unleashed in a way that makes it effective. It is possible for us to allow sin and selfishness to grieve the Spirit so that He cannot work effectively in our lives.

Being filled with the Holy Spirit is not a mystical or emotional experience. It simply means that we are being controlled by Him on an ongoing basis. We must yield to the Holy Spirit if we are to achieve God's plan for our family.

You cannot have a truly Christian home if you are walking in the flesh. Many believers are controlled by the flesh and its appetites. It is only as you yield to the Holy Spirit that you can experience the controlling fullness of the Holy Spirit which is the key to having a happy, Christian home.

A carnal man or woman is detrimental to the home. The carnal or "fleshly" Christian lives according to his will rather than God's. Walking in the flesh means that we are not living according to God's plan and pattern. A fleshly Christian will make a small problem large. A spiritual Christian will make a large problem smaller!

When we yield ourselves to the control of the Holy Spirit, He works in our hearts to change the way we act and interact in the home. There are several characteristics of a family that is surrendered to the Holy Spirit.

Surrender Produces an Attitude of Praise

Ephesians 5:19 says, *"Speaking to yourself in psalms and hymns and spiritual songs, singing and making melody in your heart to the Lord."* God's plan is that His people should praise Him. We often think of praise being confined to the Sunday worship service. But praise should begin in the heart of the home.

Fill your home with good Christian music. Teach your children to enjoy good music. Show them by example how to praise God. Throughout both Bible and church history, God's people, when they were filled with the Holy Spirit, always responded by praising the Lord.

The focus of our worship—that to which we assign value—reveals a great deal about the spirit of our hearts. Colossians 3:16 says, *"Let the word of Christ dwell in you richly in all wisdom; teaching and admonishing one another in psalms and hymns and spiritual songs, singing with grace in your hearts to the Lord."*

The words of a Spirit-filled man or woman are gracious and edifying. The Holy Spirit of God creates a disposition of grace and godliness in your family. When you are walking in the flesh, there will be words of criticism and anger, rather than praise.

Surrender Produces an Attitude of Gratitude

Ephesians 5:20 says, *"Giving thanks always for all things in the name of the Father to our Lord Jesus Christ."* Surrender to the Holy Spirit means that your home will be a place where gratitude is expressed on a regular basis. Teach your children to say, "Thank you." Teach them to express appreciation. Model this for your children.

I heard about a couple who had just gotten married. The wife was trying so hard to please her new husband. One morning she scrambled eggs for breakfast. He was not happy because the eggs were not fried. The next day she cooked fried eggs. He was not happy because they were not scrambled. So the third morning she fried one and scrambled the other. She thought surely that would satisfy him. He looked at the plate and said, "You scrambled the wrong one."

The Holy Spirit guides us and controls us to have a grateful heart. We need to stop and be grateful and thankful for what we have. Gratitude needs to be not just felt, but expressed. That may take some getting used to. Billy Sunday once said, "Try praising your wife, even if it does scare her." You will find that practicing the expression of gratitude will transform the spirit of your home.

Surrender Produces an Attitude of Submission

Ephesians 5:21 says, *"Submitting yourselves one to another in the fear of God."* It is vital that before we try to fill our roles as husbands or wives, we live up to what God has called us to be as Christians. We cannot be successful apart from God's power. You cannot be the husband or wife God means for you to be unless you are being the Christian He wants you to be. If you are not being submissive to God, you cannot hope to be properly submissive to each other.

We need to be willing to follow God's plan in every relationship, although we live in a day when people scorn submission. Our culture is not quick to acknowledge authority. We live in a day of rebellion.

In 1 Samuel 15:23, Samuel said to Saul, *"For rebellion is as the sin of witchcraft, and stubbornness is as iniquity and idolatry. Because thou hast rejected the word of the Lord, he hath also rejected thee from being king."* God is never pleased with a rebellious spirit. In fact, it repels Him from us.

God is drawn to families where the members are submitting to His divine headship over the family. God's desire is that every member of the family would be surrendered to Him. This can only happen if we are walking in the Spirit. It is not a part of our fleshly nature.

Besides possessing salvation and a surrendered heart, God desires each of us to know the security of the Christian home. This is accomplished as we acknowledge His leadership in our homes.

Security through Biblical Order

The third element of a truly Christian home is a commitment to following God's order for your family. Each member has a divinely appointed role to fulfill. Our culture does not like God's plan. Society encourages us to seek "freedom" or "fulfillment."

God wants us to have tender hearts and be submissive to Him, rather than living for ourselves. That is the foundation for a Christian home. If we are submitted to God, there will be peace in the family, even when we do not agree on things. People who are submitted to God do not rebel against each other.

I like things to be in order. I have been in some airports in foreign countries where things were in disarray. It does not give me a very comfortable feeling. I want the equipment to work and the passengers to be properly screened before I get on the plane. I want the plane to be properly maintained. It makes me nervous when things at an airport are not in order.

I also get nervous about homes where things are not in order. Such homes are headed for problems. God wants your family to be a family of order. You should not have to wonder who is in control. Some things should be distinct about the roles and relationships of a Christian home.

Husbands Are To Provide Leadership

"For the husband is the head of the wife, even as Christ is the head of the church: and he is the saviour of the body. Therefore as the church is subject unto Christ, so let the wives be to their own husbands in every thing. Husbands, love your wives, even as Christ loved the church, and gave himself for it" (Ephesians 5:23–25).

It is God's plan that the man is to be the leader in the home. This is not to be a leadership of words but of life. He is to live in such a way that he is drawing all the members of his family closer to God. I am ashamed at the way some Christian men fail to lead their families. God has placed them in that position, but they are not living up to it.

Whenever I point out God's plan for men to lead, invariably some people will respond negatively. That is because our society has a distorted view of godly leadership. Leadership is not domination; it is service. That is what Jesus taught His disciples when He washed their feet.

Being the leader means the husband is to be the first to forgive. He is to demonstrate humility, love, and concern for his wife and children. Being the leader does not mean he is a dictator who orders people around according to his whims. He is not to be harsh. Being a leader does not mean he disregards his wife's feelings or ideas.

I tell the men in our church that they should be very careful to listen to what their wives have to say. Often they have an insight into things that we, as men, lack. Men who do not listen to their wives are often missing wise counsel and great advice.

God's designation of the husband as the leader means that the final decisions rest with him. He is accountable for his family. One day he will stand before God and answer for his family. He cannot defer that leadership to his wife, his pastor, or anyone else. The man must be a leader for the glory of God in his home.

Our nation needs men who will provide this kind of leadership in their homes. God needs men to step up and fill their role in His plan. When the man of the home abdicates the leadership role, there is no security in the home.

Wives Are To Support Their Husband's Leadership

"Wives, submit yourselves unto your own husbands, as unto the Lord" (Ephesians 5:22).

Much reaction is against this one verse as any other in the entire Bible. That is partly because we do not truly understand submission.

God's plan of submission is not sexist or against women. No being in all of creation was made with greater care or attention to detail than Eve. The word *submission,* when translated, talks about order.

God's Word teaches that wives are to support their husbands' leadership. They are to be set in position under his authority. Submission is to be done "as unto the Lord." That certainly does not mean that your husband is God.

God knows that your husband will not always be right. You will not always see wisdom in his decisions. God instructs you, as a wife, to trust Him to make things work out right as you follow your husband. You can support your husband's leadership by viewing it as something you are doing for the Lord.

Men are sometimes frustrating. I heard about one lady who told her friend that the difference between *men* and *government bonds* is that government bonds *mature*. The husband is not the leader because he is smarter, wiser, or stronger. He is the leader because God placed him in that position. The wife needs to follow and support him.

Submission is not conditioned on the husband's maturity or wisdom. It is not the wife's role to manipulate her husband into doing things right. You will not always agree with your husband's decisions. They will not always be right, but you need to support him unless he wants to directly violate the Word of God.

Children Are To Obey Their Parents

"Children, obey your parents in the Lord: for this is right" (Ephesians 6:1).

God has called children to obey their parents. This is their role in the home. It is the parent's responsibility to see to it that they obey, but commanding obedience is not enough. We have to lead them in the pathway of obedience. Proverbs 23:26 says, *"My son, give me thine heart, and let thine eyes observe my ways."*

Parents need to be able to say to their children, "I want you to follow the way that I live." They need examples of what godly living looks like. We do not simply want our children's minds, we need their hearts. We need to direct them to God.

Parents need to provide direction and order in dress, entertainment, the way they shake hands, and the way children address older people. Parents need to teach respect, morality, honesty, and humility. It is the responsibility of the parents to set direction. We need to lovingly show them the way to righteousness and godliness.

Ephesians 6:4 says we are to *"bring them up in the nurture and admonition of the Lord."* At a very young age, we need to be sure the rebellious spirit is broken. As they enter their school years, we need to train and disciple them in the things of God. As they become teenagers, we need to encourage them to be actively serving God.

While children are at home, the patterns for their lives are being set. Parents need to dedicate themselves to reaching and teaching their children while they have that opportunity. Children must learn obedience to authority.

Permissiveness is destroying children. Permissiveness teaches them that their will can rule. Children cannot follow God unless they are submissive to Him, and they learn that submission in the home. Parents need to teach and model obedience to authority in their own lives.

We need God's wisdom and balance in raising a godly generation. We cannot afford to be angry or negligent. We need to demonstrate love and patience. We need to train and teach diligently. We need to base our parenting on the plan of God's Word rather than the philosophies of this world.

The sickness and moral decay we see today in America started with problems in the family. Parents have failed their children, and in doing so have failed the nation. Love your children enough to train them to obey and then enforce that obedience with tough love.

Children should obey because it is right—not because they understand, or because it makes sense to them; but because it is the right thing to do. Reasons follow obedience; they do not precede it. Teach your children to submit to authority because it is right.

Sanctity through Godly Living

"Husbands, love your wives, even as Christ loved the church, and gave himself for it; That he might sanctify and cleanse it with the washing of water by the word, That he might present it to himself a glorious church, not having spot, or wrinkle, or any such thing; but that it should be holy and without blemish" (Ephesians 5:25–27).

Finally, a truly Christian home is a place of sanctification. The members of your family are to be purified through God's Word and thereby become more like Jesus Christ. God's plan for your family is that it would be clean, holy, and pure, even in the midst of a wicked society.

Through Meditation on the Word of God

Sanctification comes through the Word of God. In John 17:17, Jesus said, *"Sanctify them through thy truth; thy word is truth."* Parents should read the Bible to their children. They should talk about the things of God. They should post Scripture verses in prominent places in their homes.

As a family, you should sing songs from the Bible together. There are even board games you can play together based on the stories and events of Scripture. Take advantage of every opportunity you have to place the Bible into the hearts and memories of your children.

When our children were young, we would ask, "Did you wash your hands?" Having boys, I learned that getting a "yes" answer did not tell me everything I needed to know. There had to be a follow up question, "With soap?" God's Word is like a detergent that brings about sanctification and righteousness. You need to make sure that your children have the soap of Scripture in their hearts and minds.

A truly Christian home centers and focuses on the Bible. Unless we make much of the Word of God, our homes will never be the sanctified place that God intends. Teach your children to make Bible memorization and meditation a part of their regular lives.

Through Moral Purity

Commit yourself to making your home a place of purity. Recently, I was talking with a pastor who told me about one of the core couples in his church. The man had gotten involved in an Internet chat room. What he justified as harmless fun in the beginning, soon turned into an adulterous affair. Before he realized the danger, his family was in ruin.

"Marriage is honourable in all, and the bed undefiled: but whoremongers and adulterers God will judge" (Hebrews 13:4).

Good families in good churches are having trouble because they are not maintaining purity in the home. You are in a battle with an enemy that is committed to the destruction of your home and family. You cannot afford to drop your guard or lower your standards.

God's will for your family is that you be pure and clean. Do not let the Devil take you down a pathway of discouragement, defeat, and humiliation. God is looking for true Christian homes—not just in name but in action. There should be a difference in your home that can only be explained by the power of God.

Many years ago, I received a letter from a young lady whose parents had once been members of our church. We did not have very many young people in those early days, but she was active in the youth group. Her family got out of church and away from God, and I had not heard from any of them in quite some time.

In her letter, she told me about the discouragement she was feeling because her parents had decided that the things of God were no longer important. They had once been active in the church and encouraged her to follow God. Now they were completely ignoring the truth they had once taught her.

She said, "Pastor Chappell, for my graduation, my grandfather gave me a Bible. I almost cried. My first thought was, 'what am I supposed to do with this?' I have never opened it since I received it. I sat it next to my old Bible, and I could not believe the difference. The old one was worn with dog-eared pages. The new one was shiny, but dusty. I think about going to church, but I can't bring myself to do it."

She went on to describe her turmoil because her mom and dad were so far away from God. Even though she was a young adult, her parents' decision to turn away from God had a devastating impact on her life. Your children, even if they are grown and out of your home, need the spiritual anchor of your godly life to help chart their courses for the future.

God has given you a plan that contains everything you need to have a truly Christian home. You will have to swim against the current of society to reach His goal, but the rewards are worth it. It is up to you to take the tools God has given in His Word and build a family that brings honor and glory to Him.

Study Questions

1. What are the four requirements for having a truly Christian home?

2. What is the most important job you have as a parent?

3. What role should the husband take in the family? the wife? the children?

4. Sanctification comes through _____.

5. List three attitudes of a family surrendered to the Holy Spirit. Which of these attitudes are most prevalent in your family? Which are least prevalent?

6. Leadership is not domination; it is service. What kind of leader are you?

7. Can you say to your children, "I want you to follow the way that I live"? Are there areas in your life that you would not want them to follow?

8. Is the Word of God the center and focus of your home? List several ways the Word of God can be used in the home to promote sanctification.

Memory Verse

Romans 8:8–9—*"So then they that are in the flesh cannot please God. But ye are not in the flesh, but in the Spirit, if so be that the Spirit of God dwell in you. Now if any man have not the Spirit of Christ, he is none of his."*

CHAPTER FOUR

Healing a Hurting Home

Likewise, ye wives, be in subjection to your own husbands; that, if any obey not the word, they also may without the word be won by the conversation of the wives; While they behold your chaste conversation, coupled with fear. Whose adorning let it not be that outward adorning of plaiting the hair, and of wearing gold, or of putting on of apparel; But let it be the hidden man of the heart, in that which is not corruptible, even the ornament of a meek and quiet spirit, which is in the sight of God of great price. For after this manner in the old time the holy women also, who trusted in God, adorned themselves, being in subjection unto their own husbands: Even as Sara obeyed Abraham, calling him lord: whose daughter ye are, as long as ye do well, and are not afraid with any amazement. Likewise, ye husbands, dwell with them according to knowledge, giving honour unto the wife, as unto the weaker vessel, and as being heirs together of the grace of life; that your prayers be not hindered.—1 Peter 3:1–7

We live in a day when marriages are crumbling. You do not need many statistics to prove that. No doubt your personal experience provides plenty of evidence. People where you work, in your neighborhood, and perhaps even in your church, or family, have been divorced.

The good news is that God has a remedy. He is the Great Physician, and He has a plan that will heal a hurting home. If you are in a situation where things are not going well in your relationship, there is hope. Do not fall into the trap of thinking there is no way out. God has provided you with the tools to save your marriage.

Christian author and family counselor Gary Smalley said he has identified two main reasons marriages seem to fail. First, men and women enter marriage with storybook expectations and limited training. He said it takes four years to get a license to be a plumber, but you can get a marriage license in about five minutes.

He once asked a young lady what she wanted in a husband. She said, "I'd like for him to be able to tell jokes, sing, and stay home all night." He replied, "You don't want a husband; you want a television set."[2]

Too many people enter marriage with unrealistic ideas of what it will be like. When reality sets in, those unmet expectations cause tremendous discouragement. As a result, one or both parties may begin to look for ways to meet their desires outside the boundaries of marriage. This is very dangerous.

Many men and women lack an understanding of the basic differences between them. To a woman, "creating atmosphere" means a nice dinner, maybe some roses, and beautiful décor. To a man, atmosphere is a big screen television and bowl of pretzels. To a woman, dressing up involves getting her hair and nails done and putting on a nice dress. To a man, dressing up is putting on a clean T-shirt. To a woman, directions are something you get at the start

---

[2] Gary Smalley, *If Only He Knew*, (Grand Rapids, MI: Zondervan Publishing House, 1979)

of a trip. To a man, they are something you get only when other people think you are lost.

Tremendous differences exist between men and women. Those differences are according to the design and plan of God. Often these differences are not apparent prior to marriage. It takes living together in the same house to bring them to light.

Because of differences and misunderstandings, spouses may become emotionally discouraged within marriage. This leads to a point of depletion and hopelessness. I have heard people say, "I just don't think this is going to work. I've lost faith in my marriage."

God designed marriage to be permanent. His plan is that your relationship will last "as long as you both shall live." Even if you are in a situation where there seems to be no hope, God has a plan to heal your hurting home. What does it take to heal a hurting home? Let's find out.

Living Humbly

"Likewise, ye wives, be in subjection to your own husbands; that, if any obey not the word, they also may without the word be won by the conversation of the wives" (1 Peter 3:1).

The Bible here tells wives to have a spirit of submission to their husbands, but submission is a two-way street. The Bible also tells husbands to be in a mutual submission to their wives (Ephesians 5:21). How is it possible for people to live this way? How can someone lay down his weapons and mutually submit in marriage?

The answer is humility. James 4:10 says, *"Humble yourselves in the sight of the Lord, and he shall lift you up."* The first step to the revival and restoration of your home is humility. You must admit that you need help and be willing to get it.

Before God

"Whose adorning let it not be that outward adorning of plaiting the hair, and of wearing gold, or of putting on of apparel; But let it be the hidden man of the heart, in that which is not corruptible, even the ornament of a meek and quiet spirit, which is in the sight of God of great price" (1 Peter 3:3–4).

Living humbly before God is an issue of the heart. Although there is nothing wrong with caring for the externals, they should not be our focus. A person who is following God must focus on the heart. Humility comes from a heart that is yielded and dedicated to following the Lord Jesus Christ

Our society is obsessed with the external. Magazines, television, and entertainment all focus on the body. I asked my wife once why the same magazine that tells you how to lose twenty pounds in thirty days also has a recipe for chocolate cake on every other page. That does not make sense.

God wants the emphasis to be on the heart. The "hidden man of the heart" is your inward self. He wants your heart to be tender and open toward Him. If your heart is hard toward God, it cannot be tender toward your family.

Because God resists the proud (James 4:6), it is only when our heart is humble that we can seek His grace and help. You must come to the place where you are willing to say, "God, I need Your help." The beginning of humility in the home is humility before God.

What does God see when He looks at your heart? Does He see pride, or a brokenness that is longing for His help in your home? When you are humble before God, it changes the way you look at everyone, including your spouse.

Before One Another

"For after this manner in the old time the holy women also, who trusted in God, adorned themselves, being in subjection unto their own husbands: Even as Sara obeyed Abraham, calling him lord:

whose daughters ye are, as long as ye do well, and are not afraid with any amazement" (1 Peter 3:5–6).

The Bible does not teach a chauvinistic domination of women by men. God's plan is for the man to be a servant leader, just as Christ washed the disciples' feet. I am the head of my home, because my wife has chosen to place herself under my leadership. When you follow God's plan, it works. We both enjoy our relationship more because we are each filling the roles God designed for us.

God wants us to be humble toward each other. Humility means being willing to defer your preferences and listen to the desires of your spouse. If your spouse sees you humbling yourself to him or her, it will greatly help repair the damages of the past.

Humility toward God must precede humility toward each other. Our fleshly nature says, "I'm first. Get out of my way." Why do husbands and wives not humble themselves toward each other? The reason is pride. Pride is the antithesis of humility.

Proverbs 13:10 says, *"Only by pride cometh contention: but with the well advised is wisdom."* If there is contention and strife in your home, it is an indication of pride rather than humility. To heal your home, you must begin by humbling yourself to God and to each other. Be willing to admit when you are wrong about something. Apologize for offenses before you are asked to do so. Take the initiative to try to make things right. Seek to find ways you can meet the needs and desires of your spouse rather than seeking your own way. Humble yourself before God and before your spouse.

Living Helpfully

"While they behold your chaste conversation, coupled with fear" (1 Peter 3:2).

Conversation refers to our manner of living or pattern of behavior. The way we live should be pure. Peter told the women in the early church that if their husbands were not saved, they could win them, not by nagging them to get saved, but by living a godly testimony before them.

Part of God's prescription for healing is that our lives are to be helpful to each other. Too often the home is a source of frustration rather than encouragement in a hostile world. One of the symptoms of an unhelpful home is that both spouses wait for the other to take the first step. That is a recipe for failure.

There is a vast difference between a thermometer and a thermostat. A thermometer merely *tells* you what the temperature is. A thermostat *controls* the temperature. Rather than simply reacting to your spouse, take an active role by doing things that will improve your relationship.

A Helpful Wife Is a Godly Wife

"Who can find a virtuous woman? for her price is far above rubies. The heart of her husband doth safely trust in her, so that he shall have no need of spoil. She will do him good and not evil all the days of her life. She seeketh wool, and flax, and worketh willingly with her hands. She is like the merchants' ships; she bringeth her food from afar. She riseth also while it is yet night, and giveth meat to her household, and a portion to her maidens" (Proverbs 31:10–15).

The Bible describes the model wife as a virtuous or godly woman, and says that she is of great value. She provides a stable environment for her husband. Since he knows that he can trust her, he is not under pressure to try to buy her affection (Proverbs 31:11). Her commitment to caring for the family frees him to play a leadership role within the community (Proverbs 31:23).

She is committed to doing good and helpful things for others (Proverbs 31:12). She rises early to make sure that the physical needs or her family—food and clothing—are met. She is an industrious and willing worker who has dedicated herself to meeting the needs of her family (Proverbs 31:21). The modern woman who does not understand God's design and plan often thinks that God wants women to be second class citizens.

Yet look at the variety of skills and talents the virtuous woman demonstrated in God's Word. This godly woman managed the affairs of a household and a staff of employees, she made clothing to sell, she was confident enough to make good decisions regarding real estate, and she planned her fields and planted crops to turn a profit. According to this inspired description, a godly woman is a far cry from second class. She has a résumé any modern graduate of Berkeley or Harvard would envy.

Being dedicated to helping your family means that you are committing to use all the talents and abilities God has given you to make your family better for His glory. If your relationship and home are hurting, take the first step by committing yourself to helpful living.

A Helpful Husband Is a Christ-Like Husband

"So ought men to love their wives as their own bodies. He that loveth his wife loveth himself. For no man ever yet hated his own flesh; but nourisheth and cherisheth it, even as the Lord the church. Nevertheless let every one of you in particular so love his wife even as himself; and the wife see that she reverence her husband" (Ephesians 5:28–29, 33).

God does not intend for the husband to be the dictator in his home. I believe God has ordained the husband to be the head of the home. God never calls a leader to exercise dominion over his followers. Rather, the greatest is the one who serves (Luke 22:25–27).

God's plan for the home is for the husband to live as Christ lived and show His love to his wife and children. The love God commands husbands to have for their wives is the same love that Jesus showed to the church—a sacrificial love. He gave Himself, willingly laying down His life for the church. That is a high standard. Yet God never commands us to do anything that is impossible to accomplish with His help. That means you can love your wife with a sacrificial love day by day.

Christ's love for the church was also a serving love. He washed His disciples' feet as an expression of humility and service. Husbands, that is the pattern that God expects you to follow toward your wife. Christ-like love does not allow marital problems to linger unresolved. Jesus did not wait for us to love Him before He poured out His life for us (Romans 5:8). Your wife may not be meeting your needs. She may not be kind or helpful in the home. Your responsibility is still to show her the love of Christ on a daily basis.

In all the years I have been pastoring and counseling couples about their marriages, I have rarely seen a man demonstrate a consistent pattern of Christ-like love without seeing his wife respond. Do not wait for her to make the first move. Act as Christ acted, stepping forward and taking the lead to be helpful to your wife.

Living Honorably

The final step to restoring a damaged relationship and healing a hurting home is bringing honor back to your home. Honor is usually one of the first casualties in a damaged relationship. Rather than treating your spouse with respect, you begin to think, and perhaps even say, unkind and cutting things.

Words have tremendous power. The words you use either build up or tear down your relationship. God's design is for families to have honor in the home. There are two key ingredients of living a life that honors your spouse.

Dwelling with Knowledge

"Likewise, ye husbands, dwell with them according to knowledge, giving honour unto the wife as unto the weaker vessel, and as being

heirs together of the grace of life; that your prayers be not hindered" (1 Peter 3:7).

Honor requires understanding. You cannot properly express honor within the home unless you understand the needs, personality, and inward desires of your spouse. To have hope for the healing of your home, you need to replace hostility with honor in your home.

ASK GOD FOR WISDOM

The differences between men and women are enormous. But in spite of those great differences, you can still understand the basic needs of your spouse. You can have this kind of knowledge by asking God. He created men and women, and He knows exactly what your spouse needs.

"If any of you lack wisdom, let him ask of God, that giveth to all men liberally, and upbraideth not, and it shall be given him" (James 1:5).

There are many things that can damage your home. Harsh and abusive words from the husband destroy the wife's desire for intimacy and fellowship. Cruel and belittling remarks from the wife destroy the husband's initiative and leadership. You can create a hard and calloused spirit with your words.

How much better it is to ask God to fill your words with understanding and grace so that they build your relationship! He will help you if you humble yourself and seek His wisdom to understand your spouse.

LISTEN

You cannot expect to bring honor to your home by dwelling with understanding unless you take time to stop and listen to what your spouse is saying. Often, in a damaged relationship, we are so intent on scoring points that we do not even hear what is being said.

"Wherefore, my beloved brethren, let every man be swift to hear, slow to speak, slow to wrath" (James 1:19).

Most of us reverse the process God has laid out for us. We are quick to speak and quick to get angry, but we are slow to stop and actually listen. It is vital that you hear what your spouse is saying instead of trying to justify yourself. If you go into a defensive mode, you will miss the opportunity to learn and grow in your marriage.

When you listen, focus all of your attention on what the other person is saying. It is easy for me to plan the next oil change for the car while my wife is talking. This is not true listening. Even if you can repeat the words she said, you are not listening if your mind is somewhere else. Being "swift to hear" means being fully focused on listening.

Knowing the needs of your spouse is critical to healing your home. A wife needs affection. To a woman, affection is not an event, it is an environment. She is looking for expressions of love as a way of life, not just occasionally when you want something. She needs to feel secure.

I saw a sign in a florist's window once that said, "Smoking or forgetting your wife's birthday can be hazardous to your health." God created women with different needs than men. Men need to listen to understand what their wives need.

Husbands need approval from their wives. So often a couple will come in for counseling and, within minutes, the words the wife uses to describe her husband reveal contempt and aggravation rather than approval. Men who do not receive approval at home are dangerously vulnerable to the temptation to look for approval outside of the marriage.

A wife is wise to listen to her husband's needs. She needs to try to understand the way God created him. Men tend to focus on external things, which is often frustrating to their wives. Remember that God designed you differently for a reason. Take the time to listen to each other, so that you can restore honor in your home.

Dwelling with Respect

You can restore honor in your marriage through respect. Disrespect is like an acid that eats away at the fabric of your relationship. If you want to receive respect, you have to sow respect by building up your spouse.

WITH OUR ACTIONS

"Finally, be ye all of one mind, having compassion one of another, love as brethren, be pitiful, be courteous" (1 Peter 3:8).

The way we treat each other should bring glory to God. Colossians 3:17 says, *"And whatsoever ye do in word or deed, do all in the name of the Lord Jesus, giving thanks to God and the Father by him."* Can you treat your spouse harshly in the name of the Lord Jesus?

I like to see a husband who has been married for twenty years still holding the door open for his wife. That may be a small thing, but it is a visible demonstration of respect. Good manners and courtesy go a long way toward strengthening your relationship. Respect tells your spouse that you think he or she is worthy of first class treatment.

Examine your actions in light of the fact that God sees everything you do. Is He pleased and honored by the way you treat your spouse? Are you demonstrating respect or contempt in the way you treat each other?

WITH OUR WORDS

"Not rendering evil for evil, or railing for railing: but contrariwise blessing; knowing that ye are thereunto called, that ye should inherit a blessing. For he that will love life, and see good days, let him refrain his tongue from evil, and his lips that they speak no guile" (1 Peter 3:9–10).

Do not say hurtful or wicked things to your spouse. Do not talk about things that your spouse cannot change. Do not compare your spouse to others to point out his or her shortcomings. You cannot have healing in your home if the words being spoken are bitter and painful.

The words you use reveal what you truly think about your spouse. Make sure that your words are building your relationship rather than tearing it down. Colossians 4:6 says, *"Let your speech be alway with grace, seasoned with salt, that ye may know how ye ought to answer every man."*

Salt is a preservative. Having your speech be "seasoned with salt" means that your words should preserve honor, not destroy it. Do not say anything that will damage the honor and respect in your home. If you want to have a family that lives honorably, your speech must reflect respect for your spouse.

You may have reached a point where you feel it is impossible for your marriage to be restored. I want to encourage you to remember that nothing is impossible with God (Matthew 19:26). No matter what depths your relationship has reached, it can be rescued if you are willing to follow God's plan.

God has given us a prescription for healing a hurting home. You can make the decision today to follow God's plan. Ask God to help you restore humility, helpfulness, and honor to your home, and watch Him transform your relationship.

Hearing this plan from God's Word is like getting a prescription from the drug store. One of the most important things a pharmacist will tell you is to "take all the medicine." Some people try to pick and choose only a small portion of what God says is needed. You need to do all that God directs in order for your marriage to be healed.

I believe any marriage can be transformed with thirty days of right living. Ask God to change you rather than asking Him to change your spouse. You cannot expect the effect of accumulated offenses to be forgotten overnight. But as your spouse sees a new lifestyle on your part, he or she will begin to respond. In time, God will restore your marriage and satisfy the deep needs of your heart.

Study Questions

1. What does it take to heal a hurting home?

2. The beginning of humility in the home is _____.

3. How can a husband/wife live helpfully?

4. To honor your spouse, you must dwell with what two things?

5. Pride is the antithesis of humility. What are some ways to reconcile the damage of pride in your marriage?

6. What is the difference between a thermometer and a thermostat? Which one are you?

7. When was the last time you really listened to your spouse? How can you improve your listening skills?

8. Are you in the habit of using kind words or hurtful words?

Memory Verse

1 Peter 3:8—*"Finally, be ye all of one mind, having compassion one of another, love as brethren, be pitiful, be courteous:"*

PART TWO

Priorities for Your Children

CHAPTER FIVE

Developing the Heart of Your Child

But Daniel purposed in his heart that he would not defile himself with the portion of the king's meat, nor with the wine which he drank: therefore he requested of the prince of the eunuchs that he might not defile himself.—Daniel 1:8

*Shadrach, Meshach, and Abednego, answered and said to the king, O Nebuchadnezzar, we are not careful to answer thee in this matter. If it be so, our God whom we serve is able to deliver us from the burning fiery furnace, and he will deliver us out of thine hand, O king. But if not, be it known unto thee, O king, that we will not serve thy gods, nor worship the golden image which thou hast set up.
—Daniel 3:16–18*

I do not know who you want to meet when you get to Heaven, but there are some people who really rank high on my list. I would like to get to know Moses. I would like to spend time talking to the Apostle Paul. I would really like to meet Daniel's parents and the parents of Shadrach, Meshach, and Abednego.

I would like to talk to them about how they instilled such character into the hearts of such young men. Daniel and the three Hebrew children were great men of God as teenagers. Without a doubt, those parents were successful in developing the hearts of their children.

It is the responsibility of parents to bring their children up *"in the nurture and admonition of the Lord"* (Ephesians 6:4). Every parent who reads this book would no doubt agree that it is a giant task requiring God's help.

Children are a gift from God! They are not ours. They belong to Him. God knew Jeremiah and had a plan for his life even while he was in his mother's womb (Jeremiah 1:5). Knowing then that our children are so important, we must do everything we can to develop their hearts for God.

God has a special plan for the life of each of your children. Every plan is different and uniquely suited to the talents and abilities He has given to those young people. Our responsibility as parents is to ensure that our children find and follow God's plan for their lives.

Let's discover how these teenage young men came to make the right decisions for God. The key to the whole story of Daniel and his friends is found in the expression *"Daniel purposed in his heart"* (Daniel 1:8). The heart is where the critical issues of life are decided (Proverbs 4:23).

All of us who are parents should commit ourselves to rearing young people like Daniel and the three Hebrew children. It is a great tragedy when children are reared without a tender heart for God.

All children are going to sin and make mistakes. They are going to face challenges and choices, and sometimes they will choose wrongly. The problem I see today is that Christian young people sin and feel no remorse or conviction. The greatest tragedy is not that they sin; but that they do so without a realization of the effects of that sin on themselves, others, and their relationship with God.

If our children do not feel convicted and burdened about sin, we have failed them as parents. Through my years as a pastor, I have noticed a hardening of Christian young people toward sin. This reveals that they do not have tender hearts toward God.

The book of Daniel is a success story. It shows us how young men, even in difficult circumstances, can keep soft hearts for God. Today we tend to blame rebellion and sin on bad circumstances. A bad family life, bad economic circumstances, or bad conditions do not justify bad behavior.

With God's grace, your child can have a heart for God despite any circumstances he experiences. Daniel faced a terrible situation as a teenager. A wicked king named Nebuchadnezzar led the armies of Babylon against Jerusalem. In a raid on the capital city, they carried away the prime young people of Judah.

Daniel and his friends were taken to Babylon and held against their will. This was a common practice of the Babylonians. They would take promising young people from conquered nations and indoctrinate them in the Babylonian system. These young men were trained for Nebuchadnezzar's wicked purposes.

Daniel and the three Hebrew children were outstanding young people. They were among the choice young men taken from Jerusalem. They were forcibly taken from their families into a wicked environment. Yet for all its wickedness, Babylon was at the same time a very attractive environment.

These young men must have found that the environment in Babylon was awesome to behold. Babylon held one of the wonders of the ancient world—the Hanging Gardens, built by Nebuchadnezzar. Babylon was home to phenomenal architecture, music, and science. It was the cultural, political, and military center of the world. Imagine being a teenager, ripped away from your family and placed into such an awe-inspiring environment.

Imagine, also, the temptation to a teenager. He is being flattered and told he is one of the best and brightest. If he will just go along with the system and cooperate, he will receive position, prestige, and power. Daniel and his friends could have received everything the world had to offer if they had just gone along with the program.

All they had to do was change their diet a little. That seems like such a small thing. Can you imagine the pressure on them to conform? Can you imagine how they must have felt being separated from family and being so far from home? Yet these four young men withstood every temptation they faced.

The fact that Daniel, Shadrach, Meshach, and Abednego stood firm is an indication that we can succeed as we work to rear our children to be faithful to God. We can develop their hearts so that they will seek and serve Him, regardless of what comes into their lives.

We know that our children will have bumps in the road along the way. Not one child from our families is perfect, but there can be a process of development that will prepare them for confrontation by the world. When their faith and convictions are challenged, they will have the tools to make right decisions and honor God.

They can have a heart that is sensitive to God so that when they are away from us they will still make the right decisions and stand for what is right. So how can we as parents develop that kind of heart in our children?

We Must Develop a Purposeful Heart

Daniel *"purposed in his heart"*—Daniel 1:8. This tells us that before he faced temptation he had made up his mind to live for God no matter what the consequences were. A young person who has a purposeful heart is one who has made the decision that he is going to follow God.

Purpose Begins at Salvation

The greatest decision in life is to accept Jesus Christ as Saviour. That is the beginning of having a heart for God. This is just as true for our children as it is for us. Saving for your child's college education or sending them to a prestigious school is not the most important preparation you can make for your child's future.

The greatest thing we can do is teach them God's plan of salvation. We cannot make the decision to accept Christ for them, but we can teach them truth from the time they are very small— that they are sinners, that there is a penalty for sin, that Jesus paid that penalty, and that there is no way to Heaven except trusting Christ as Saviour.

In 2 Timothy 3:15, Paul said to Timothy, *"And that from a child thou hast known the Holy Scriptures."* It is a blessing when children are saved at an early age. We should teach them about God during their developmental years.

At salvation, the Holy Spirit of God comes to indwell the person who receives Christ. *"But ye are not in the flesh, but in the Spirit, if so be that the Spirit of God dwell in you. Now if any man have not the Spirit of Christ, he is none of his"* (Romans 8:9). Having the Holy Spirit enables our children to know the purpose of God in their hearts and follow that purpose.

A man without Christ cannot even know the purpose of God, let alone follow it. If our children are to have purposeful hearts toward God, they must have the presence of God in their lives. When I accepted Christ as Saviour, I did not understand every aspect of the spiritual transaction that took place.

It would be years before I understood the doctrine of sanctification and other aspects of the miracle of salvation. But at the moment I prayed and asked God to save me, the Holy Spirit took up residence in my life. He began teaching and helping me.

Have I always listened to Him? No, but I have the potential to walk in the purpose and plan of God because the Spirit is in my life. Leading our children to Christ at an early age offers them that same power.

I heard a story about a little boy who was out flying his kite. It was a windy day, and the kite kept going higher and higher. Finally it got so high that it was out of sight. A man passed by and saw the little boy holding onto the string. The man could not see the kite, and he asked the boy, "How do you even know you have a kite up there?" The boy replied, "Because I can feel it."

I believe that when a child is saved, he begins to sense the presence of the Holy Spirit of God in his life. That indwelling presence, convicting and encouraging a child, enables him to develop a purposeful heart.

Purpose Is Developed through the Word of God

As young children learn from God's Word, they begin to find the purposes of God for their lives. Solomon explained the role of teaching based on God's Word when he said, *"He taught me also, and said unto me, Let thine heart retain my words: keep my commandments, and live"* (Proverbs 4:4).

It is critical that you read the Word of God to your children. When they are old enough, teach them to read it, daily, on their own. Encourage them to commit verses of Scripture to memory. To some people, hearing young people quote verses is just rote memory work that has no meaning. To those who believe what God's Word says about itself, it is the very core of true education for life.

God's Word gives a young person purpose and direction for living. *"Thy word is a lamp unto my feet, and a light unto my path"* (Psalm 119:105). Teach your child the principles and commandments of the Bible. Your child cannot have a close relationship with God without knowing about Him. The way we learn about God is through His Word. The Bible reveals God's character, nature, desires, and plans for our lives. Our children will not be able to follow His purpose without a personal knowledge of His Word.

It is very unlikely that children will develop a personal relationship with the Bible unless they learn it from their parents. Children value what their parents value. If you model the importance of Scripture in your life, your children will also learn to value it.

Purpose grew in Daniel's heart because a mom and dad in Jerusalem followed God's instruction and taught him the Scriptures at a young age. They gave him a heart for God and His Word, which gave purpose and direction to his life.

Terrie and I have tried to encourage our children to purpose to serve God. They have served through the evangelism outreach of our church, in ministries such as the bus ministry or teen soulwinning. They have volunteered at the hospital and served in the campaigns of good politicians. At Christmas time we have annually hosted the widows of the church, and our children have served. We have tried to show them that life's purpose is greater than serving self.

We Must Develop a Pure Heart

Daniel purposed that *"he would not defile himself"* (Daniel 1:8). He was committed to purity. No matter what threats or rewards were offered, Daniel refused to be tainted with the philosophy of Nebuchadnezzar. His heart was pure and true toward God.

A Pure Heart Leads to Pure Living

First Peter 1:22 says, *"Seeing ye have purified your souls in obeying the truth through the Spirit unto unfeigned love of the brethren, see that ye love one another with a pure heart fervently."* God's Holy Spirit and the Word of God work together to purify our hearts.

Daniel had a pure heart. As a result, his life was pure. This is what Jesus was talking about in Matthew 5:8 when He said, *"Blessed are the pure in heart: for they shall see God."* The word *pure* means cleansed. We are purified when we accept Christ as Saviour, but we also need a daily cleansing as we walk through a dirty world.

The Bible provides this cleansing. Jesus prayed for His followers in John 17:17, *"Sanctify them through thy truth: thy word is truth."* The heart must be clean if the life is to be clean. No amount of focus on cleaning the outward life can compensate for a lack of holiness in the heart.

"Woe unto you, scribes and Pharisees, hypocrites! for ye make clean the outside of the cup and of the platter, but within they are full of extortion and excess. Thou blind Pharisee, cleanse first that which is within the cup and platter, that the outside of them may be clean also" (Matthew 23:25–26).

God expects us to be good representatives of Him in this wicked world, and holiness always begins on the inside. We must teach our children to guard their hearts and keep them clean and pure.

Proverbs 15:8 says, *"The sacrifice of the wicked is an abomination to the LORD: but the prayer of the upright is his delight."* God takes pleasure in the prayers that are offered by those who have pure hearts. Developing pure hearts in our children prepares them for close, intimate, and effective relationships with a holy God.

Daniel and his friends had such a relationship with God. They applied the Holy Scriptures, the part that was available to them, to their lives. The book of Daniel is a continued illustration of how pure hearts are unwilling to disobey any Bible principle. No threat of danger or reprisal could force those young men to disobey God, because their hearts were pure toward Him.

Daniel attributed his deliverance from the den of lions to inward purity. *"My God hath sent his angel, and hath shut the lions' mouths, that they have not hurt me: forasmuch as before him innocency was found in me; and also before thee, O king, have I done no hurt"* (Daniel 6:22). When God looked into Daniel's heart, He saw "innocency"—purity.

A Defiled Heart Leads to Defiled Living

What we believe determines how we behave. In Titus 1:15, Paul said, *"Unto the pure all things are pure: but unto them that are defiled and unbelieving is nothing pure; but even their mind and conscience is defiled."* When we talk about developing our children's hearts to be tender toward God, we must be on guard to protect them from being defiled.

The word *defiled* means to be "unclean, stained, polluted, contaminated, or smeared with mud." Why can two children grow up in the same home with the same parents and hear the same truths taught, and yet respond so differently? The Bible tells us that it is based on what is in their hearts.

We are living in a day in which children's hearts are being defiled through entertainment and television. They are being defiled through friendships that pull them away from God. Children are being defiled through worldly philosophies they pick up in school.

Unfortunately, many moms and dads are defiling their children by exposing them to sin in the home. Too many of us are willing to excuse "little" sins like gossip, bitterness, anger, or dishonesty in ourselves. When children see a double standard lived out before them, they develop a cynical attitude toward the things of God.

As a result, the child sees everything as defiled because his heart is defiled. But when someone's heart is pure, he sees things as pure. I have seen that demonstrated in a church setting, especially with young people. I was preaching from the life of Saul once, and I read the story of how he was out looking for his father's donkeys.

Of course, the King James Bible uses the word *ass* for donkeys. When I read that verse, most people did not react at all. But a few teenagers snickered and thought it was funny. Why were they responding like that? Because to a defiled heart, everything is defiled.

As a parent, you must pray that God will help you keep your own heart clean and right and guard your children's hearts so that they will be pure on the inside. The most important thing we can do for our children is to rear them with pure hearts. This will protect them from the pitfalls that the Devil will place in their way.

A person with a defiled heart judges everyone else through the paradigm of his own defilement. Dr. Bob Jones, Sr. once spoke of a man who was complaining that preachers only cared about money. "What he means," Dr. Jones said, "is that if he were a preacher, that would be his motive." Pure-hearted people do not think the worst about everyone; they hope for the best.

As a parent, you cannot depend on anything or anyone else to develop the hearts of your children. I am thankful for every good youth group, but a youth group will never take the place of parents. I am thankful for every good Christian school, but the responsibility for your child's heart cannot be handed off to a principal or a teacher. You must do everything you can to guard his heart from being defiled. You can make no greater investment in your child's future than to keep his heart clean and pure and tender toward God.

We Must Develop a Principled Heart

The reason Daniel and his friends never wavered from doing what was right is that they had committed themselves to living by principles. In Daniel 3, we see the story of Daniel's three friends, Shadrach, Meshach, and Abednego's refusing to worship the idol Nebuchadnezzar had built.

> *Then Nebuchadnezzar in his rage and fury commanded to bring Shadrach, Meshach, and Abednego. Then they brought these men before the king. Nebuchadnezzar spake and said unto them, Is it true, O Shadrach, Meshach, and Abednego, do not ye serve my gods, nor worship the golden image which I have set up? Now if ye be ready that at what time ye hear the sound of*

the cornet, flute, harp, sackbut, psaltery, and dulcimer, and all kinds of musick, ye fall down and worship the image which I have made; well: but if ye worship not, ye shall be cast the same hour into the midst of a burning fiery furnace; and who is that God that shall deliver you out of my hands? Shadrach, Meshach, and Abednego, answered and said to the king, "O Nebuchadnezzar, we are not careful to answer thee in this matter. If it be so, our God whom we serve is able to deliver us from the burning fiery furnace, and he will deliver us out of thine hand, O king. But if not, be it known unto thee, O king, that we will not serve thy gods, nor worship the golden image which thou hast set up.—Daniel 3:13–18

These young men were committed to their principles. They would not worship Nebuchadnezzar's idol even when threatened with a painful, agonizing death. They would not bow down to a false god. They had been taught as young children that there were principles in the law of God that were to be followed no matter what.

My goal for my children is that they grow up to be men and women of principle. These young Hebrew men had grown up with convictions that were unshakable. They had spiritual maturity. It did not matter where they were; they were going to do right. That is what principled living is all about.

Learn Principles from God's Word

Living by principle is not conditioned on age. It is conditioned on learning and obeying the commandments of Scripture. Paul told the church at Ephesus to, *"Be ye therefore followers of God, as dear children"* (Ephesians 5:1). Your children, even while they are very young, should begin to live lives that are dictated by obedience and not convenience. The only way to live by principle is to adhere to the Word of God.

Principles of dignity, modesty, honesty, and integrity are not out of date. God still expects you to teach your children according to the precepts of His Word. These young men withstood the pressures of compromise because they had been trained from a young age to love and serve God.

Your children need to see that their parents are following God with a child-like heart. They need to see you living according to the principles of the Bible and demonstrating the Christian life before their eyes. You must have a principled heart so that you can pass it on to them.

"And God spake all these words, saying, I am the Lord thy God, which have brought thee out of the land of Egypt, out of the house of bondage. Thou shalt have no other gods before me. Thou shalt not make unto thee any graven image, or any likeness of any thing that is in heaven above, or that is in the earth beneath, or that is in the water under the earth: Thou shalt not bow down thyself to them, nor serve them: for I the Lord thy God am a jealous God, visiting the iniquity of the fathers upon the children unto the third and fourth generation of them that hate me;" (Exodus 20:1–5).

This is the first of the Ten Commandments—not the Ten Suggestions. God is serious about our living according to His ways, not our own. We must teach our children what is right and wrong in their youth.

The three Hebrew children had learned this principle from their parents. They were facing tremendous peer pressure—all around them were thousands who were bowing down. They said to the king, "We're not bowing down, even if you throw us into the furnace." They had learned the precepts of God's Word, and they held to them.

The Word of God has the power to shape and mold our lives and our children's lives to make them pleasing to Him. When we teach our children to apply the principles of the Bible, we give them the tools they need to stand against temptation and sin.

Model Principles in Your Family Life

A principled heart must be developed in our children while they are young. The way to accomplish this goal is for us to model principles, personally. How can we expect children to care about modesty if parents do not? How can we expect children to care about purity if parents do not? We need to live by principles and model this kind of life before our children.

In the early days of my ministry, I sometimes jumped into teaching on outward standards of separation too soon. Standards regarding modesty and Christian testimony are important, and I want our people to have them and keep them. However, I do not want to merely pastor a church that has outward standards. I want to pastor a church where the members live by principles that are based on the Word of God. Standards are just an extension of the principles. They are not an end in themselves.

We need to take the same approach with our children. Many parents focus on making sure their children do right and tow the line, but they stop there. As long as the kids are outwardly compliant and not making waves, they are happy.

It is good and important for your children to do right, but that, alone, is not enough. They need to learn the underlying principles, not just the guidelines that enforce those principles. I believe the reason many Christian families see their young people turn away from God after they leave home is because their children only learned the outward rules and not the inward principles.

"With my whole heart have I sought thee: O let me not wander from thy commandments. Thy word have I hid in mine heart, that I might not sin against thee" (Psalm 119:10–11).

Giving our children principles grounded in God's Word and modeling those principles before them prepares them to live a life that pleases God. We must give them these principles ahead of time so they will be ready to face the challenges and temptations to come.

Before our sons, Larry and Matthew, enter a new school year, I will talk to them about avoiding situations in which they might be tempted to do wrong. I challenge them to let their peers know early that they love God, and want His will for their lives.

The average child who has adopted the world's philosophy says, "If it feels good, do it." The principled child who has adopted the precepts of the Bible says, "If it's according to the Scriptures, do it." The difference is not in the temptation. It is in the heart of the child.

Hundreds of young men were taken from Jerusalem to Babylon. The ones who adapted to the system, accepted the new philosophy and diet, and turned their backs on God, are now lost in the mists of time. The names of the four who stood for God are still remembered today.

Your child can have that kind of heart for God. You can succeed as a parent. You can commit and dedicate yourself to developing the heart of your child to be tender toward God. I challenge you, today, to make that decision and devote yourself to carrying it out. It will shape the destiny of your descendants for generations to come.

Study Questions

1. What kind of heart should you strive to develop in your children?

2. When should you begin teaching your children God's Word?

3. A pure heart results in what kind of a relationship with God?

4. Where can children learn godly principles?

5. Children value what their parents value. How can you model the importance of Scripture in your life?

6. What can you do to nurture your child to develop a pure heart and protect him from a defiled heart?

7. Are your children's lives and actions dictated by obedience or convenience?

8. Is your heart pure, purposeful, and principled? Do your children see it?

Memory Verse

John 17:17—*"Sanctify them through thy truth: thy word is truth."*

CHAPTER SIX

A Biblical View of the Family

When we saw the World Trade Center towers crumble on September 11, 2001, we realized that there were threats in the world we had not been aware of before. We were shaken out of our complacency and brought face to face with some harsh new realities. While it took about six years and eight months to build the trade towers, it only took about one hour and forty-two minutes for them to fall down.

The crumbling of families is a devastating issue in America. While it took many years to develop a strong nation with biblical convictions on which strong families can be formed, it has taken a relatively brief amount of time for the family to disintegrate in America.

Immorality, illegitimacy, and divorce have changed the social structure and moral landscape of our country. Many of you reading this have suffered through family difficulties and trials. If you have gone through heartache, it is not my intention to reprimand you.

What I want to do is to help give you the tools to make your family work. I want you to learn what God designed the family to be. I want to show you how following His plan will protect you from the chaos striking families all around us.

The source of great problems within our society is crumbling families. Karl Zinsmeister of the American Enterprise Institute said, "We talk about the drug crisis, the education crisis, the problem of teen pregnancy, and juvenile crime. But all these are traced back to one predominant source: broken families."[3]

There is also a link between healthy families and a healthy economy. Writing in *Foreign Affairs* magazine, Daniel Yankelovich said, "The success of a market-based economy depends on a highly developed social morality."[4] What he meant was that trustworthiness and honesty are cornerstones of the economy.

If you do not believe this, just look at the history of big businesses—recent illegal activity at WorldCom, Enron, Adelphia Cable, and Tyco has shown us what happens when business leaders do not possess basic moral values. A lack of moral fiber is affecting every part of our country. Every social ill of our day has some connection to the disintegrating family.

Problems in every venue of life can be traced back to problems in the home. Many people do not want to face this because it means they have to take personal responsibility. We often hear people blame society for their problems. The truth is that society is just a collection of families. If those families are not following God's plan, chaos will result.

God's Design for the Family

From the beginning of creation, God had a clear purpose and plan for the family. Just as the builders of the World Trade Center started with a blueprint before they began construction, God has a

---

[3] Karl Zinsmeister, *Marriage Matters* (The American Enterprise: May/June 1996)

[4] Daniel Yankelovich, *Foreign Policy After the Election* (Foreign Affairs Magazine: Fall, 1992)

pattern and design, revealed to us in His Word, for what he wants your family to be.

The Family Provides Companionship

"And the Lord God said, It is not good that the man should be alone; I will make an help meet for him. And the Lord God caused a deep sleep to fall upon Adam and he slept: and he took one of his ribs, and closed up the flesh instead thereof; And the rib, which the Lord God had taken from man, made he a woman, and brought her unto the man" (Genesis 2:18, 21–22).

God designed us to need each other. As we look at ourselves, we realize that we have a deep need for friendship and companionship. There is an old saying, "Joy shared is multiplied; sorrow shared is diminished." God specifically designed Adam and Eve to meet the needs He knew each of them had.

I believe in a God who has the power to create. His creation works when we follow His plan. Because there has been a dearth of sound Bible teaching and preaching, too many people, even Christians, do not know God's plan. Others know it but are not willing to follow it. Marriages are in trouble around us.

Someone once said to me, "Many girls marry a man just like their fathers. That is why so many mothers cry at weddings." We have lowered our expectations and allowed the failures of marriages in our society to set our expectations for Christian homes. From the beginning, God had a high ideal of marriage.

Marriage was instituted by God to fulfill our deepest needs for companionship.

The Family Provides Completion

God intended that two—husband and wife—would become one. God's design is that their differences would complement each other and complete what they were lacking. God knows our individual needs. Your family, when living according to God's design, will meet the physical, emotional, and spiritual needs that you have.

"Therefore shall a man leave his father and his mother, and shall cleave unto his wife: and they shall be one flesh" (Genesis 2:24).

God intends for your marriage and family to be complete and permanent. There are times in any relationship when some needs are not being met. If you are not careful, those cracks in the foundation can lead to collapse. After years of counseling couples, I have come to realize that every marriage faces seasons of trials—times when we wonder, "What is going on?"

Good marriages take work. This must be a priority item. God does not want you to develop other areas of life at the expense of this primary relationship. Your marriage is important. Work at it. Take the time to improve it. Find ways in which you can become better at meeting the needs of your spouse.

God does not intend for you to find your source of fulfillment through your job, bowling league, or an Internet chat room. He intends for you to find it with your spouse. Every time you get this "out of whack"—whether you are a preacher, an engineer, or a homemaker—problems come. We cannot depart from God's design for marriage and expect good results.

You must make the commitment to know and follow God's design. His purpose, plan, and view of marriage is found in the Bible, and it does no good to know what God's plan is if we do not do it (James 1:22)!

The Family Provides Continuation

FAMILY MULTIPLICATION

One of the purposes for your family, according to the divine plan of God, is to continue the human race by having children. It is important to note that even before the fall of man, children were part of God's design.

"So God created man in his own image, in the image of God created he him; male and female created he them. And God blessed them, and God said unto them, Be fruitful, and multiply, and replenish the earth, and subdue it: and have dominion over the fish of the sea, and over the fowl of the air, and over every living thing that moveth upon the earth" (Genesis 1:27–28).

Our culture no longer highly values children. Every decade, we murder millions of them before they are even born. The Bible teaches us that children are a special blessing and gift from God (Psalm 127:3). We need to view them and treat them as such.

As Christian couples, we should be thankful when God gives us children and realize that they are part of His plan for the family. Frankly, it concerns me to see so many Christian couples who do not have any desire to have children. They have allowed the world's philosophy to influence their thinking rather than desiring to pattern their families after God's purpose.

FAMILY DISCIPLESHIP

According to God's design, the home is to provide more than just a source of children to continue the human race. We are to train our children to know and love God. The home is to be the center of teaching Bible truth to the next generation.

"And thou shalt love the Lord thy God with all thine heart, and with all thy soul, and with all thy might. And these words, which I command thee this day, shall be in thine heart: And thou shalt teach them diligently unto thy children, and shalt talk of them when thou sittest in thine house, and when thou walkest by the way, and when thou liest down, and when thou risest up" (Deuteronomy 6:5–7).

From the beginning of a child's life, the family is the place where discipleship is to happen. The home is the place where children are to learn to love God. It is the place where children are to see models of the love of God in the lives of a loving mother and father. Without these models at home, where will they learn to be good husbands or wives? The home is to be the place where children learn God's design for marriage.

Parents do not need to have a "church service" for an hour each day at home. Terrie and I have enjoyed beginning the day with our children by reading Scripture, and then asking our children questions from the Scripture. We also share prayer requests, and sometimes sing a song.

The process of discipling our children can sometimes be a little slower than we wish it would be. I heard about a father who was looking over a report card. It contained straight A's. The boy said, "Dad, you told me to bring home a good report card. So I brought home Billy Wilson's report card."

Every parent sometimes feels like the kids are just not getting it. Do not throw in the towel. Do not give up. Keep on teaching. Keep on training. Keep on disciplining. Get in their faces if you need to. Go out and have a Coke with them if you need to. Do whatever it takes to train your children to follow God. God's design is that the family will fill this role.

I pastor a church where the Bible is taught and preached. We do everything we can to train and equip parents to rear their children. You need to be in a church like that. It is not primarily the church's job to teach your children to love God—it is your job. Your family needs to be a discipleship center for your children. Every home should be a mini-Bible institute where the Word of God is taught on a daily basis.

The World's Departure from God's Design

Satan knows that the Christian home is at the center of God's plan for His creation. He fully understands that if he can undermine the home, he will wreak havoc on future generations. He has perfected a weapon to unleash against the family—the curse of promiscuity and immorality.

"Flee fornication. Every sin that a man doeth is without the body; but he that committeth fornication sinneth against his own body. What? Know ye not that your body is the temple of the Holy Ghost which is in you, which ye have of God, and ye are not your own? For ye are bought with a price: therefore glorify God in your body, and in your spirit, which are God's" (1 Corinthians 6:18–20).

The world system around us glamorizes immoral behavior. Television, movies, music, and books promote a false picture of sex. God designed sex as a good thing within marriage. It is part of His plan. Within the boundaries of marriage, we do not need to be ashamed of the good thing God created.

Far too many Christians, today, are seeking to meet sexual needs outside of marriage. Immorality always damages a marriage relationship. In a society where anything goes, everything eventually will. We must recognize that the world is rapidly going away from God's plan.

"For this is the will of God, even your sanctification, that ye should abstain from fornication: That every one of you should know how to possess his vessel in sanctification and honour; Not in the lust of concupiscence, even as the Gentiles which know not God" (1 Thessalonians 4:3–5).

Sometimes people tell me that it is hard to figure out what God's will is. Frankly, it is usually pretty plain. These verses make it abundantly clear that God's will is for us to remain pure. Fornication is any sexual relationship outside of marriage, and it is never part of God's design.

The world's plan for sexual fulfillment is everything except marriage. We are bombarded on all sides by a culture that is obsessed with sex, and the results are painfully obvious. There are one million illegitimate babies born each year in the United States. That statistic does not take into account the hundreds of thousands of abortions.

Why are we seeing this moral calamity? Because families are not following God's plan. Parents are not teaching their young people to be clean and pure and to save themselves for marriage.

In 1992, when then Vice President Dan Quayle tried to stand for stable, two-parent families, he was made a laughingstock. He stood up against illegitimacy on television. He was right. His point was also largely ignored. The rate of illegitimate births increased 60 percent in the 1990s.

Single parent families are not what God's original plan intended. You may be reading this book as a single parent. I am not saying that you are inferior, nor am I saying that you cannot succeed. There are many single parent families in our church where moms or dads are doing a great job of raising their children without spouses. I am sure they would be the first to tell you that it is a constant struggle. It is hard enough to rear godly children with two parents devoting themselves to the task. I have a tremendous respect for those good people who are trying to make the best of a very difficult situation.

The success of the world's attack on God's design for marriage ripples through every part of our society. Sadly, the statistics on divorce and immorality among people who profess to be Christians is basically the same as it is among those who do not. This is a tragic failure.

These sins are impacting our young people, as well. In his excellent book, *Moral Dilemmas*, J. Kirby Anderson reported that teenage girls' natural desire for male companionship is heightened when they are reared without fathers. That fact, combined with teenage insecurity, often leads to immoral behavior as girls seek to replace what they are missing from God's plan with the Devil's substitute.[5]

There is a direct correlation between broken families and the increase in illegitimacy. Unfortunately, our government has joined

---

[5] J. Kirby Anderson, *Moral Dilemmas* (Baker Book House: 1997)

the act and actually encourages immoral behavior. I have counseled dozens of couples who are living together outside of marriage. Repeatedly I have been told, "If we get married, we'd lose our check from the government." It is a real problem when the government rewards bad behavior.

Illegitimacy creates a cycle of dependency and anger. Daniel Patrick Moynihan wrote an article entitled "Toward a Post-Industrial Social Policy." He said that in 1950, 52 percent of black children and 81 percent of white children lived in a family with both parents until they reached 18. In the 1990s those figures were 6 percent and 30 percent respectively.[6]

Families are crumbling because of immorality. Too many parents—even Christian parents—have bought into the world's lie and have given up on their marriages. This is devastating to our young people. They are emulating the immoral behavior they see in the lives of their parents.

Broken homes lead to broken hearts and cultural decline. America has not followed God's plan. We are reaping a bitter harvest as a result. Too often we forget that the Devil's purpose is to destroy God's plan for the family.

The fruit of immorality is not fun. It involves broken hearts, broken relationships, and broken homes. As parents we have a responsibility both to teach our children moral behavior and to show it to them as well. They need to learn from us that culture is often wrong and God is always right.

Your children need to see that two people can love each other and be faithful to each other. They need to know that they do not have to give in to immoral pressures. They need to know that "everybody isn't doing it."

Today things are getting worse as we see the push for homosexual marriage. This is nothing more than another front in the Devil's attack on God's design for marriage and families.

---

[6] Daniel P. Moynihan, *Toward a Post-Industrial Social Policy* (The Public Interest, Summer 1989)

Two men or two women living together is sin, not marriage. No matter how many court rulings are issued approving this ungodly and immoral behavior, marriage will always remain the union of a man and a woman. In Leviticus 20:13, the Bible says, *"If a man also lie with mankind, as he lieth with a woman, both of them have committed an abomination...."*

The world is doing everything it can to break down God's plan, and it will only get worse for our children. Knowing this, we have to commit ourselves to train, disciple, and ground them so they will know right from wrong and have the courage and tools to swim against the tide of cultural decay that surrounds us.

The Decisions of Strong Families

Families that determine to live according to God's plan in today's environment have to make certain decisions and set down guidelines to follow. The basis for these decisions is the Word of God. Nothing else will enable us to survive and train our children to stand against a culture that is diametrically opposed to God.

Follow Biblical Principles for Marriage

Tens of thousands of Christian families in America are not following God's principles for marriage. They are believers, in some cases actively involved in their churches, but they are not living out their marriage relationships according to God's Word.

Although there are a multitude of Bible principles for your home, I want to focus in this chapter on just two that need to be guiding principles for your marriage. You need to irrevocably commit to living by these principles.

CHRIST-LIKE LOVE
This kind of love only comes as the result of a decision. Committing to Christ-like love means that no matter what happens, how bad

things may become, or what troubles come, we are going to love each other like Jesus loves us.

In Ephesians 5:25, Paul wrote, *"Husbands, love your wives, even as Christ also loved the church, and gave himself for it."* He is talking about the kind of love that is a giving, caring, considerate love. It is a sacrificial, need-meeting love.

I have had dear friends in the ministry who become so involved in meeting ministry objectives that family needs are not being met. You can be involved in something as important and noble as keeping people out of Hell, but if you are not meeting the needs of your family, you are missing God's plan and design. We must meet the needs of our families. This is not optional. Your spouse and children need to be a priority.

In his best-selling autobiography, Lee Iacocca wrote: "Hard work is essential. But there is also a time for rest and relaxation, for going to see your kid in the school play or at a swim meet. And if you don't do those things while the kids are young, there's no way to make it up later on."[7]

Stop and look at your schedule. Where are you spending the majority of your time? Is the importance you place on your spouse and children reflected on your personal digital assistant? Are you demonstrating Christ-like love by meeting their needs ahead of your own? If not, you need to decide to make some changes in your life.

GODLY FAITHFULNESS

To fulfill God's design for your marriage, you must have an unshakable commitment to the sanctity of your marriage. Your marriage vows are absolute.

"Marriage is honourable in all, and the bed undefiled: but whoremongers and adulterers God will judge" (Hebrews 13:4).

---

[7] Lee Iacocca with William Novak, *Iacocca* (New York: Bantam Books, 1984, page 289)

God is not pleased with sexual promiscuity outside of marriage. Do not allow yourself to be swayed by the prevailing trends in our culture or the false belief that "everybody's doing it." Not everybody is doing it, and even if they were, that would not excuse you from your marriage vows.

God regards faithfulness in marriage as being critical. He is not willing to settle for less. His plan is for the husband and wife to be one flesh without anyone else ever coming between.

We must be faithful to our marriages. We must stand guard against temptation. We must be watchful and vigilant, because the Devil is seeking to destroy marriages. Above all, remember that your children are learning powerful lessons about morality as they watch your behavior.

Teach Abstinence to Your Children

"For this is the will of God, even your sanctification, that ye should abstain from fornication" (1 Thessalonians 4:3).

We need to explain to our children that they are to wait for a physical relationship until they are married according to God's plan. I hear parents say, "It's hard to talk about." Talk about it anyway. You should not be embarrassed or ashamed to explain God's plan to your children.

They need to learn about sex from you rather than from friends, teachers, or our perverted culture. They need to know that sex is God's design within marriage. Do not be guided by what happened when you were young. Things have changed. Young people today have been exposed to so much more than we were. They need the *truth* before they are faced with the choice.

Stand on what the Bible says. Explain the biblical reasons for complete abstinence and the consequences of immorality. Your children need to know about the lifetime of pain and problems if they violate God's clear command for purity before marriage.

You may be familiar with the True Love Waits Campaign. In this campaign, young people are asked to sign a commitment which I think is an excellent summary statement of God's purpose.

> Believing that true love waits, I make a commitment to God, myself, my family, those I date, my future mate, and my future children, to be sexually pure until the day I enter a covenant marriage relationship.

This should be your goal and dream for every one of your children. Purity affects every part of their future. It affects their future spouses, children, and of course, it has a tremendous impact on them, personally. How many people have I counseled who said, "I wish I had waited." I have never had someone tell me they were sorry that they had remained pure.

Fathers Accept Their Responsibility

Not far from where I pastor there is a state prison. On any given day there are between 4,000 and 6,000 inmates there. According to the statistics, 78 percent of those men were raised without a father.

God's plan is that dads have to be involved with their children. In Ephesians 6:4, Paul said, *"And, ye fathers, provoke not your children to wrath: but bring them up in the nurture and admonition of the Lord."* Fathers who accept their responsibilities to their families are the keys to the success of God's design for marriage.

It is not enough "not to leave." Dads have to accept their responsibility to be involved. They need to be fully engaged—emotionally, physically, and spiritually—with their wives and children. They need to be the leaders of the home.

Many people I counsel are angry at God because they had absent, angry or abusive fathers. Children largely form their understanding of God from their relationships with their dads. If they do not see a model of the faithfulness and love of God from their fathers, it is hard for young people to accept the truth about God.

They need to see loving, nurturing faithfulness. They need to hear, "I love you" from their dads. They need to hear, "I'm sorry" when dad is wrong. Fathers are essential to the molding and shaping of children to be mature followers of Jesus Christ. There is no other alternative to replace your committed involvement with your children.

Dads need to model faithfulness in the home. They need to be faithful to their wives, children, work, churches, and in their neighborhoods. This is a vital commitment to the success of your family.

We live in a world that has abandoned God's view of what a family is supposed to be. We live in a world in which successful marriages are too rare, but the Holy Spirit gives us the power to overcome the world. We can succeed at building a family according to God's design and plan, if we are willing to commit to building according to the blueprint found in His Word.

Study Questions

1. What is the source of the greatest problems in our society?

2. The family is to provide what three things?

3. In light of the world's departure from God's design, what do your children need to see?

4. What is Christ-like love?

5. Husband and wife, are you providing the companionship and completion that meets the other's needs? Are there things you need to honestly talk through to make your relationship better?

6. Have you made a decision to have a strong, God-honoring family?

7. Are you teaching your children about God's plan for marriage, or are you letting the world do it?

8. Dad, do you say "I love you" and "I'm sorry" in the home?

Memory Verse

Genesis 2:24—"*Therefore shall a man leave his father and his mother, and shall cleave unto his wife: and they shall be one flesh.*"

CHAPTER SEVEN

The "Three Rs" of a Spirit-Led Family

In no arena do we need God's direction more than in the arena of the Christian family. Allowing the Holy Spirit to lead your family in today's world is a real challenge. A pastor friend of mine told me about something that happened in his church. There was a six-year-old boy sitting with his father in church. The little boy was acting up and wiggling. The dad kept telling him to be quiet, but the boy got louder and louder.

Finally, the dad picked the boy up and started to walk out. It caught the attention of many people. The boy noticed the eye contact and said, "Pray for me! Pray for me!" The pastor said he lost the service for a few minutes. It was pretty hard to get people's attention back on the message after that.

We certainly do need prayer, and God's help for our families. The home stands at the center of civilization. The great need of our time is for Spirit-led Christian homes. A home is not Christian because the parents have their names on a church roll or because religious pictures are hanging on their wall.

A true Christian home is a place in which the family members are following the leadership and direction of the Holy Spirit of

God. It is a place in which the Word of God is read and prayers are offered up. It is a place in which people are trying to show the Spirit of Christ in their daily relationships. How can we ensure that we have that kind of home?

Foundational Roles

The first key to establishing and maintaining a Spirit-led home is Christian parents who have yielded themselves to the Lord. If the parents are not playing their part, there is no possibility that the home will be what God intends for it to be. For years, Dr. Lee Roberson has used the saying, "Everything rises and falls on leadership." He is exactly right.

Parents Are To Fill the Role of a Godly Authority

Parents are to be obeyed. Often in today's society, we see roles completely reversed. We see children dictating what they want to do; what they want to wear; and what they want to watch on television. The Bible says that God's plan is for children to obey.

More than a daughter needs her mother to be her best girlfriend, she needs a mother who is a spiritual authority. More than a son needs a good buddy, he needs a dad who is a spiritual leader in the home. Parents must step up and fill the role of godly authority.

In his book, *Shepherding a Child's Heart*, Tedd Tripp said, "The problem today is not that kids don't want to receive authority; it is that parents don't want to take authority."[8] Children need direction and guidelines from their parents. The problem is that too many parents are not willing to do the work of establishing rules and making them stick.

Many times we see fathers become indifferent and abdicate the leadership of the home. It is easier to let mama run things, so the dad shrinks back, and the wife is forced to assume a place that

---

[8] Tedd Tripp, *Shepherding a Child's Heart* (Wapwallopen, PA: Shepherd Press, 1995)

God did not intend her to fill. Men need to step forward and accept responsibility rather than transferring it to their wives.

That is why Ephesians 6:4 says, *"And, ye fathers, provoke not your children to wrath: but bring them up in the nurture and admonition of the Lord."*

Many parents are throwing in the towel because it is so difficult to enforce rules in a culture that questions authority and glorifies rebellion. We must not yield to the culture. That is not the direction we get from God's Word.

"Hear ye children the instruction of a father, and attend to know understanding. For I give you good doctrine, forsake ye not my law. For I was my father's son, tender and only beloved in the sight of my mother. He taught me also, and said unto me, Let thine heart retain my words: keep my commandments and live" (Proverbs 4:1–4).

Many dads did not grow up in homes with fathers who taught them. There were no family devotions in the home. Their dad never taught them about discipline or godly convictions. As a result, many dads are having to "learn on the job" the things they need to know to fulfill the role God has given them.

Do not give up on succeeding! Do not go back to the way things were before you decided to follow God's pattern. I challenge you to fulfill your role as the godly authority in your home.

Sometimes it is difficult to explain Scripture to our children. Someone asked me recently, "How do you have family devotions with a three-year-old?" I replied, "Very briefly." You need to use wisdom and discernment and not give them more than they can handle. Establish in their very earliest memories that God's Word is true and that they can count on their parents to give them instruction that is Bible-based.

I heard recently about a boy who was going through the family photo album with his mother. Looking at one picture he asked, "Mom, who's this man on the beach with you with all the muscles and the curly hair?" She said, "Well, that's your father." He said, "Well, then who's the old, bald-headed guy who lives with us now?"

We may be diminishing physically. We may not be able to do the things we used to do. As someone said, our narrow waists and broad minds may have switched places. However, we should be growing spiritually every day. We should be getting stronger, living more like Jesus, and becoming more mature in our Christian faith. This is what our children need to see in our lives.

"Hearken unto thy father that begat thee, and despise not thy mother when she is old. Buy the truth, and sell it not; also wisdom, and instruction, and understanding. The father of the righteous shall greatly rejoice: and he that begetteth a wise child shall have joy of him" (Proverbs 23:22–24).

Our desire should be to raise up children who have a righteous heritage. A godly authority is critical to reaching that goal. Parents, do not give up. Do not cede it to the television. Do not give it to a relative. Do not even try to pass it off to a youth group or Christian school. They can help, but God has given the primary responsibility to you. Like it or not, you are to be the primary authority in the lives of your children.

Parents Are To Fill the Role of a Godly Example

It is not enough to be an authority figure who says, "Do what I say, not what I do." Many parents are like that today. They smoke, but tell their kids not to. They drink, but tell their kids it is bad for them. They take the kids to church, but drop them off instead of going themselves. This kind of parenting simply does not work. We must be able to say, "Follow me."

This is the model Jesus practiced with the disciples. He said, *"…follow me, and I will make you fishers of men"* (Matthew 4:19). We cannot expect to lead our children to a place of victory if we are not experiencing it ourselves. In Ephesians 6:4, the Bible says that we are not to *"provoke our children to wrath."* One of the primary ways parents exasperate their children is by living a double standard. We must be an example to them in the home.

I have received dozens of letters over the years from kids who were bitter and angry at their parents. They were struggling with issues because they had seen a difference between what their parents said in public and what they lived in private. It is a tragedy when the home is not a place of safety and godly examples.

When I think of the right kind of example, I think of the life of Timothy. In 2 Timothy 1:5, Paul said, *"When I call to remembrance the unfeigned faith that is in thee, which dwelt first in thy grandmother Lois, and thy mother Eunice; and I am persuaded that in thee also."*

Timothy's father was not a Christian man, but his mother and grandmother raised him up in the ways of God. They gave him examples he could follow. Even if you are a single parent, or your spouse is not a believer, you can still give your children a godly example of faithfulness to follow.

It is also important to realize that after your children become adults, they are still watching your testimony. They are looking to see if you really meant those things you taught them. They need to see you demonstrate how to work through mid-life and old age and still be following Jesus Christ.

We need to be faithful examples. In Philippians 4:9, Paul said, *"Those things, which ye have both learned, and received, and heard, and seen in me, do: and the God of peace shall be with you."* That is what a faithful example is—it is a person whose walk and talk match. It is more than words. It is showing, not just telling.

Our children watch us constantly. They see what is really important to us. They need to see that the things of God matter more to us than the things of this world. They need to see that God is a real and vital part of our lives every day.

We were all saddened when the space shuttle *Columbia* disintegrated. But I was encouraged to learn that two of the astronauts were wonderful Christian examples. Rick Husband and

Mike Anderson were members of the same church in Texas. Before they made that last flight, they made a video for their church. That video was played at their memorial service.

Astronaut Rick Husband, captain of the *Columbia* mission, said on that video, "If I ended up at the end of my life having been an astronaut, but having sacrificed my family along the way, or living my life in a way that did not glorify God, then I would look back on it with great regret. Having become an astronaut would not really have mattered all that much."

He was at the pinnacle of his career. Only a few dozen human beings have ever left Earth for space. Thousands of people apply to NASA every year, and only a handful are accepted. In spite of all that he had accomplished, he said that if he did not pay attention to his family, he would have missed what really mattered. That is a faithful example his children will be blessed to follow. They will miss him until they are reunited in Heaven, but thank God that they have the memory of that kind of father.

We need to be consistent examples. If parents have a different opinion on a matter, they need to resolve it in private—not in front of the children. Authority is so important in the eyes of a young child. God ordains authority (Romans 13:1–7), and if we tear down any authority in a child's presence, all authority will be diminished in his eyes.

Satan is doing everything he can to put doubts in the mind of children about authority. At our Christian school we ask all the parents to sign a pledge that they will support the school. If they have a question, we ask that they come to the administration in the right spirit and ask it. That pledge is really not for the parents. It is for the benefit of the children. The point of the pledge is so that the children will see a united front between the authorities in their lives. They need to see them working together. Parents need, to the best of their ability, to provide a consistent example.

Fulfill Responsibilities

The second key to having a Spirit-led home is to fulfill the responsibilities God has assigned to us as parents. This is where the actual work of parenting takes place. It is not hard for people to agree that parents should be the authority in the home and set the example. That is basic. The question is, how do we actually accomplish this? What does God expect us to do, as parents?

We Are To Nurture our Children

We are to train our children and bring them up. It is our responsibility to prepare them for life. We are to give them instruction and guidance. Proverbs 23:26 says, *"My son, give me thine heart, and let thine eyes observe my ways."* In Proverbs 29:15 we read, *"The rod and reproof give wisdom: but a child left to himself bringeth his mother to shame."*

The French philosopher Jean-Jacques Rousseau was one of the earliest advocates of the idea that children are naturally good. He felt that discipline and training corrupted the innate goodness of the "natural savage." His argument was that society taught evil to children. Of course, he also abandoned his five children to an orphanage, refusing to be involved in their upbringing.

His ideas quickly took root, and still exert a great influence even today. This approach appeals to a humanistic world, but it is in direct conflict with the Word of God. Proverbs 22:15 says, *"Foolishness is bound in the heart of a child; but the rod of correction shall drive it far from him."*

Foolishness is not something children learn. Psalm 58:3 says, *"The wicked are estranged from the womb: they go astray as soon as they be born, speaking lies."* We must give our children guidance in the paths of righteousness from their earliest days.

If you choose to follow the advice of our world and let your child find his own way, you will have shame (Proverbs 29:15). Children are crying out, even in their most rebellious moments, for a parent to say, "This is what we believe and we're going to stand by it." Even when they are pushing you, they will respect the fact that you are holding the line.

Give them the wisdom, advice, and direction they need, even when they do not understand it. You do not have to wait; indeed you should not wait until they can fully comprehend everything. Start with small guidelines when they are young, and you will find that they are more easily directed as they grow.

The English poet, Alexander Pope, wrote, "As the twig is bent, so grows the tree." If you have ever had new trees planted at your house, you are familiar with the stakes that are put into the ground beside the tree. The stakes are there for a purpose—to train the tree to grow straight and tall.

Those stakes work remarkably well if they are put in place when the tree is young. But if crooked growth has been allowed to develop for several years, they will not be effective. Rules for our children work the same way. God expects us to put guidelines in place while they are young (Proverbs 19:18), so that they will grow to love and obey Him.

We Are To Admonish our Children

To admonish is to warn our children about what is wrong and encourage them about what is right. The relationship between the child and the parents is critical to development and maturity, and God has given fathers a special role that is often neglected.

I encourage single mothers to find positive male influences and role models for their children. Kids need dads. But the Devil knows that, too. So he is directing an all-out attack on male leadership in the home. It seems like almost everything in our culture and popular entertainment is geared toward tearing down fathers.

In 2003, James Dobson called attention to this attack on fathers in his newsletter. He quoted the lyrics from one of the top songs of 1953, "Oh, My Papa" by Eddie Fisher.

Oh, my papa, to me he was so wonderful.
Oh, my papa, to me he was so good.
No one could be so gentle and so lovable,
Oh, my papa, he always understood.
Gone are the days when he would take me on his knee,
And with a smile, he'd change my tears to laughter.
Deep in my heart, I miss him so today,
Oh, my papa. Oh, my papa.

Of course, families had problems then just like they do now. Fathers were not perfect. But can you imagine a song like that even being released today, let alone being the most popular song in the country?

Things began to change in the 1960s. The "generation gap" came into place. Tension erupted between the generations. Some of you, no doubt, remember the slogan of the Youth International Party—the Yippies, "Never trust anyone over 30."

In 1984 the rock group, *Twisted Sister*, had a hit song that talked about fathers too. It was called, "We're Not Gonna Take It." The lyrics of that song referred to a father who was called a "disgusting slob" who was "worthless and weak." The song ends with him being blasted out of a second story window.

The Devil is doing everything he can to drive a wedge between parents and children. The authority in many homes today is not parents, but MTV, the most popular cable channel in the world. It reaches into more than 230 million homes in over 75 countries. It promotes material that tears down godly values, moral standards, and parental authority.

Many of the problems that plague our families today can be traced to the venom that is being piped into our homes via the television. Josh McDowell published a survey a few years ago of 3,700 Christian teenagers. Nearly 50 percent of them admitted that they watched MTV on a daily basis.

I cannot stress strongly enough to you that MTV is your enemy, and it is your children's enemy. The sooner you figure that out and

cut off the pipeline of evil, the better off your family will be! Deal
with it. Do whatever it takes. Our country needs parents who are
willing to stand up and identify sin!

We often have parents visit our church in Lancaster. They want
to know if the nursery is sterilized and the toys are clean. They want
to know if the workers are competent and have passed background
checks. But many of those same parents who are worried about
protecting their kids at church are letting them contaminate their
minds at home with MTV.

We Are To Teach Principles to our Children

It is the parents' responsibility to teach godly principles of behavior
to their children (Deuteronomy 6:5–7). We need to talk to our
children about our growth and spiritual walk. We need to tell them
about what we have read in our Bible study and devotional times.
They need to know that God is real to us. Lift up the things of God
to your children.

It is critical that you have these principles in your own life
before you can teach them to your kids. You need to know *why*
you believe what you believe so you can pass it on to them. It is so
important that we teach the next generation how to live their lives
according to God's principles.

We must get beyond "because Dad said so" in teaching them
why sin is wrong. Many kids get the right details (like no MTV), but
the parents never teach them the reasons for the rules. So when
they get out on their own, there is no basis for their beliefs. It is
then easy for kids to abandon their parents' rules because they have
no foundation of their own.

Here are some practical guidelines to develop standards
of protection for your kids. It does not take a village—it takes a
mommy and a daddy. We have to stop depending on others to raise
our children and get back to the precepts of the Word of God.

BEGIN WITH A BIBLE PRINCIPLE

Whatever we believe about righteous living and walking as a spiritual family should begin with a Bible principle. It is not what we say, but what the Bible says that matters. The eternal, unchanging Word of God has power and authority. And we need to read and study it so that we will know what God says about the issues we face and how we should live.

DEVELOP A CONVICTION

A conviction is a personal belief based on a Bible principle. Once we have identified a principle, we need to follow the leading of the Holy Spirit to develop guidelines for our lives. These are rules you have decided to follow to ensure you will obey the principles of the Word of God. Not everyone will come to the same convictions, but you, as parents, need to determine how your family will follow God's instructions.

ESTABLISH A STANDARD

A standard is a guideline that helps me keep my conviction. There is nothing wrong with having standards in your family. That seems strange to people who do not have any standards. But godly standards will not hurt your children. In fact, they prepare them for life in the real world.

There are standards in every industry. Last year I was invited to speak at a church that was just beginning. One of our church members works for United Airlines, and he offered to let me use a Buddy Pass to keep down the travel expenses. When he gave me the pass, it came with some guidelines. You could not wear shorts, flip-flops, or denim. Those were the standards of United Airlines.

Now I did not have a problem with that. I did not walk onto the plane and tell the pilot I should have been able to wear blue jeans. I did not tell him he was a "legalist!" The standard was set, and I was willing to comply.

Here is an example of how the process of establishing standards should work. Psalm 101:3 says, *"I will set no wicked thing before mine eyes: I hate the work of them that turn aside; it shall not cleave to me."* That is a Bible principle that shows us how we should live. On the basis of that principle, I have come to a conviction for myself that I will not watch or read anything wicked. That conviction helps me follow the principle God expects me to uphold, which is laid out in Psalm 101:3.

Then I have established a personal standard to help me keep that conviction. For example, I will not watch HBO or MTV. That standard is connected to the conviction, which is connected to the Bible principle. It is not arbitrary or a matter of preference. It is there for a reason. The point of the process is for our children to understand the reasoning behind the standards.

By establishing standards in this way, I can pass on principled living to my kids. I give them, not just rules, but the principles that are the foundation for the rules. Teaching principles in this way also prepares them to live and make decisions on their own.

There are a lot of things the Bible does not specifically address. It does not say anything about HBO or MTV. But it does say not to set wicked things before our eyes. We need to teach our children to discern the principles so they can deal with those things that are not specifically addressed.

It is your responsibility, as a parent, to develop convictions and standards based on the Word of God, and then instill them into your family so that your children will know and understand the direction. Teach your children to live by principle.

Foster Relationships

Finally, if we are to have a Spirit-led home, we must establish and maintain good relationships with our children. Someone wisely has said, "Rules without relationships bring rebellion." As you begin to fulfill your role as the authority in the home and teach your children, make sure that you take time to express your love for them.

Spend time with them. Do whatever is necessary to keep the relationship intact. Your children have to know that you care about them, and that they are a priority in your life. You cannot fake what is important to you. They will know if they are not in the right place on your priority scale.

I heard about a little boy, named Johnny, who showed up late for Sunday school one morning and was looking very sad. His teacher was concerned, and said, "Johnny, what's wrong?"

"Well, I was going to go fishing today, but Dad said I needed to go to church."

The teacher was impressed, and asked Johnny if his dad had explained to him why it was important for him to go to church instead of going fishing.

Johnny replied, "Yes, teacher, Dad said he didn't have enough bait for both of us."

Relationships Are Built through Time Together

First Peter 3:7 says, *"Likewise, ye husbands, dwell with them according to knowledge."* This verse is talking about the husband-wife relationship, but the same principle applies to our children. The word *dwell* means to settle down in a fixed place. We must spend time together to build vital relationships.

There are no shortcuts to building a relationship with your children. You can only do it by investing time in them. In *A Passion for Excellence,* Tom Peters, a management expert, had some comments on the time priorities our world values.

> We are frequently asked if it is possible to 'have it all'—a full and satisfying personal life and a full and satisfying, hard-working professional one. Our answer is: No. The

> price of excellence is time, energy, attention and focus,
> at the very same time that energy, attention and focus
> could have gone toward your daughter's soccer game.
> Excellence is a high cost item.[9]

Tom Peters is right—you have to make choices. But I hope you will not make the choice he recommends. You need to determine that your children are important enough for you to make sacrifices for the sake of your relationship with them. This will cause them to know how important they are to you.

It gets harder as they get older. Many parents do well until their children become teenagers. Then they allow the busyness and increased activities to come between them and their children. You have to make plans, on purpose, to spend time with your family, especially as your children grow.

Being a pastor of a growing church has been quite demanding at times. But Terrie and I have worked diligently to make family memories. When our girls turned thirteen, we took them to fancy dinners and presented them with their own purity rings. On their sixteenth birthdays we took them out for a memorable dinner and then had a nice party with their friends. Every summer for sixteen years we have gone with our kids to see the Dodgers play a time or two. We have enjoyed amusement parks, national parks, and simple nights at home.

Relationships Are Built through Talking Together

"For I was my father's son, tender and only beloved in the sight of my mother, He taught me also, and said unto me, Let thine heart retain my words: keep my commandments and live" (Proverbs 4:3–4).

God wants us to communicate with our kids. His plan is that we talk to them. There is no substitute for parents talking to their children. The power of family stories is tremendous. That was one

---

[9] Tom Peters and Nancy Austin, *A Passion for Excellence* (New York: Random House, 1985)

of the keys to the success God's people had in building character in their children.

It is amazing to look at the lives of young people like Joseph, Daniel, and the little girl who was taken captive to Syria by Naaman. Even though they were very young when separated from their families, they remained true to the God of Israel. I believe this was due to their training, which included an emphasis on the stories of God's working with their ancestors.

Our children have cell phones. I make it a practice to call them up and leave messages for them. I want them to hear from me even when we cannot be together. I tell them I am praying for them. I encourage them to do what is right and behave as children of God should behave. They need to know that I love them and am concerned about what is happening in their lives.

Talking with your children is a two way street. It is not just you talking to them. It is also listening. Their concerns and burdens are very real. They need someone who listens and takes them seriously. There is no way to schedule when a serious conversation will take place, so you must be ready and willing to drop what you are doing to listen when they have something to say.

Use every means you can to communicate. Develop your relationship with your children. Spend time talking and listening to your children. When you do, you are investing in their futures.

Having a home that is led by the Spirit of God depends on having parents who meet their foundational God-given roles, parents who fulfill their responsibilities, and parents who foster strong relationships with their children. These are the homes that succeed. This is the kind of home you can have by God's grace.

Study Questions

1. What is the definition of a true Christian home?

2. What are the "three R's" of a Spirit-led family?

3. How can you develop standards of protection for your children?

4. What are the two ways to build a parent/child relationship?

5. How can your family devotions improve to be more effective for your family?

6. What do you need to change in your life to be the role model God wants you to be for your children? What are you doing that you don't want them to imitate?

7. Are you starting to guide your children at a young enough age?

8. What is the greater influence in your home—you or the television?

Memory Verse

Proverbs 23:26—*"My son, give me thine heart, and let thine eyes observe my ways."*

CHAPTER EIGHT

Fight for Your Children

And Judah said, The strength of the bearers of burdens is decayed, and there is much rubbish; so that we are not able to build the wall. And our adversaries said, They shall not know, neither see, till we come in the midst among them, and slay them, and cause the work to cease. And it came to pass, that when the Jews which dwelt by them came, they said unto us ten times, From all places whence ye shall return unto us they will be upon you. Therefore set I in the lower places behind the wall, and on the higher places, I even set the people after their families with their swords, their spears, and their bows. And I looked, and rose up, and said unto the nobles, and to the rulers, and to the rest of the people, Be not ye afraid of them: remember the Lord, which is great and terrible, and fight for your brethren, your sons, and your daughters, your wives, and your houses.—Nehemiah 4:10–14

Although he was a foreigner, Nehemiah had a position of great trust in his office as cupbearer to the king of Persia. He was greatly burdened when he received a report about the conditions in which the Jews who had gone back to Jerusalem were living. So Nehemiah asked for and received permission to return to rebuild the wall around the city.

The wall was both a literal and a symbolic protection. Nehemiah had both a burden and a vision. That vision was for more than just building a wall. He recognized that the wall was necessary for worship to continue in the temple that was being rebuilt and for the people to remain safely in the city.

Great adversity came during the process of building the wall. Opposition came from without by the people who had moved into the area during the captivity. Opposition also came from within. The people of the tribe of Judah, the largest of the tribes, became discouraged by the challenges.

Nehemiah recognized that what they were doing was not just for themselves; it was for future generations. The rebuilding of the wall was something that would have impact for years to come. Nehemiah had a vision for the future.

I believe that when Nehemiah challenged the people of Israel to fight for their sons and daughters, he was reminding them of the vital fact that the battles they faced were changing the lives of future generations.

As a parent, I am constantly reminded of the fact that raising children is more about the future than the present. They are growing and developing in their faith, but my job is not done yet. I believe this is the most important responsibility God has given me. I pastor a great church filled with wonderful people, but the biggest job I have is as a father, not a pastor.

I realize that my children are not growing up in an easy time. The world of my childhood was a very different place than the world in which my kids live. Some of the things we are seeing today would never have been seen when I was young.

We did not hear cursing or see immorality portrayed on television. It was unknown to hear music on the radio filled with cursing and sexual innuendo. Today, there is a constant battle. An all-out war is being waged against our children.

Nehemiah recognized there was a battle in his day, not just for the people he was leading, but also for the next generation. It is the same for you. Our children and grandchildren will fall if we do not win the battle. We cannot afford to put our lives in neutral and coast.

If the Lord does not return, our children will have to live in a world that is opposed to everything we are trying to teach them. I want to leave my children some remnant of morality and godliness to help them succeed. If we lose this battle, if we lay down our swords, how will our children have a chance?

God has ordained the home. It is His plan and design. It was not invented by society. It is not a product of evolution. It was not created by the courts or the legislature.

Children are part of God's design for the home as well. God's plan is for you and your spouse to work together to teach and train your children to love and follow Him. Each one of your children is a gift from God. Your son or daughter is a living soul created by God. You have a responsibility to influence his or her heart toward God.

You cannot alter the mind, will, and emotions with which your child was created. What you can do is influence and shape the mind, will, and emotions by your godly leadership in the home. You are not God, but you do have the ability to influence them toward God.

Philippians 2:13 says, *"For it is God which worketh in you both to will and to do of his good pleasure."* He is the One who does the life-changing work and gives the will to do right. We need to commit to play our roles and do our parts.

My prayer is that when my children leave home and have families of their own, they will continue to make godly decisions.

One of the most important things I can do for them is demonstrate, now, the kind of lives I pray they will lead as adults.

I have seen committed, godly parents have problems with their children. I have seen good people who tried hard, yet their kids are wayward. Sometimes kids do go astray. I do not always understand why. I have seen young people in our church in every setting—public school, Christian school, home school—turn away from God. It does not matter what the atmosphere is; it matters what is in their hearts.

Going to church will not save your kids. Reading the latest best-seller on parenting will not save your kids. Using the newest techniques will not save your kids. Your heart, as a parent, must be right with God. So many people think there is a formula that will guarantee no problems with children. Winning the battle for their hearts is the way to succeed as parents.

Fight Your Own Spiritual Battles

"Take heed unto thyself, and unto the doctrine; continue in them: for in doing this thou shalt both save thyself, and them that hear thee" (1 Timothy 4:16).

Before you put a plan in place to work on your children, you must stop and take a look in the mirror. Timothy had great responsibilities as a pastor. He may well have had many churches to oversee. Yet, Paul told him to first ensure that he was guarding his own life before he focused on those other responsibilities.

It is a tragedy when a parent is not tending to his own heart. Before you fight to defend your children, fight the battle within your own heart. A man once told his congressman, "I believe we should put prayer back in the public schools." The congressman replied, "I'm a Christian, and I agree with you. But let me ask, did you pray with your children at home this morning?"

One of the real problems with Christians, today, is that we have loud mouths about every one else's problems, but we are not taking care of the issues of our own hearts. It is much easier to focus on the outward, but the key battle lies within.

Parents, you are responsible, first, for your direction. Ultimately, as they become adults, you are not responsible for your children's direction. It is true that you are responsible for the influence you have on them. You have a responsibility to bring them up in the nurture and admonition of the Lord. You can influence the set of their sails, but they are responsible for their own decisions as adults.

One of the greatest needs of our society is that we quit blaming our parents for the things we do wrong. Sigmund Freud introduced the concept of determinism to society. It was well received. The idea that we can blame every sin or failure on someone else is attractive. The problem is this idea is completely false and contrary to the Word of God.

"Know ye not, that to whom ye yield yourselves servants to obey, his servants ye are to whom ye obey; whether of sin unto death, or of obedience unto righteousness? But God be thanked, that ye were the servants of sin, but ye have obeyed from the heart that form of doctrine which was delivered you. Being then made free from sin, ye became the servants of righteousness" (Romans 6:16–18).

Recognizing that we are personally responsible to God is critical to our success as Christians and as parents. How, then, can we win the battles in our own lives so we can influence our children for God and right?

Focus

You must have the right focus to win your spiritual battles. Over the years I have done quite a bit of hunting. One of the first things you have to do with a new gun is make sure it is sighted in. You need to know you have your weapon focused so you can hit your target.

"Wherefore seeing we also are compassed about with so great a cloud of witnesses, let us lay aside every weight, and the sin which doth so easily beset us, and let us run with patience the race that is set before us, Looking unto Jesus the author and finisher of our faith; who for the joy that was set before him endured the cross, despising the shame, and is set down at the right hand of the throne of God" (Hebrews 12:1–2).

Looking unto Jesus means that we are making Him our focus. The Devil has many ways to ruin your children. One of the best is to get you as a parent off focus. If the father backslides or the mother becomes bitter, it has a powerful influence on the children. You cannot focus on other people or problems and win battles.

In Nehemiah's day, the people of Judah were focused on the rubbish. They allowed the problems to cloud their vision for what the building of the wall would mean to their children. Keep the focus on your personal relationship with Jesus. Do not lose sight of Him.

A story is told about a man who visited the construction site of one of Europe's great churches. He asked one worker what he was doing. "I'm laying bricks," came the reply.

He asked the same question of a second worker. "I'm building a wall," that man said.

The third worker he asked, unlike the first two, had a vision for his task. When he asked what he was doing, he replied, "I'm building a cathedral." Having a clear picture of what we are doing is critical to victory in our personal spiritual battle.

Faithfulness

Make the determination that, no matter what happens, you are going to be steadfast, unmovable, always abounding in the work of the Lord (1 Corinthians 15:58). Commit to it. Do not waver from your determination. Do not let anything turn you aside.

There will be times when you do not want to do the things you know are right. Make the commitment that, even when you do not feel like it, you are still going to do right. One of the keys to spiritual victory is your decision to be faithful to God and to your family.

Be faithful to God's Word. In 2 Timothy 2:15, Paul told Timothy, *"Study to shew thyself approved unto God, a workman that needeth not to be ashamed, rightly dividing the word of truth."*

Over the years in counseling, people often have said, "Pastor, I haven't been in the Word of God like I should. Pray with me that I'll get back into the Bible." I always do, but I do more than just pray. I urge them, as strongly as possible, to get back into the Word.

If you are not faithful in reading and studying the Scripture, you are leaving the door wide open to failure in your own life. You will dry up, spiritually, unless you are spending time in the Bible regularly.

Your children need to know that the Bible is a priority in your life. They need to see you read it, and hear you talk about it. They need you to model to them a faithfulness to the Word of God.

Fervency

"Not slothful in business; fervent in spirit; serving the Lord" (Romans 12:11).

There are too many passive Christian parents in our day. You must stay actively involved in your home. You must stay actively involved in the church. Be fervent in every role in your life.

On May 19, 1643, John Winthrop established the New England Confederation. Their constitution clearly laid out their purpose. It said, "To advance the kingdom of our Lord Jesus Christ…To preserve and propagate the truth and the liberties of the Gospel."

The founders of our country were loyal to Jesus Christ. They had a desire to raise up a nation for their children and their children's children; they had a spirit that would not stop. They were not willing to settle for passive living. We need that spirit back today. We need it in our homes and churches.

Do not just go through the motions. I have known some good preachers over the years who were actively involved in the work. Then they got weary. They lost their zeal and fervency. Today some of those men are no longer in the ministry. If you lose your fervency, you will end up on the sidelines instead of in the battle for your children.

Fight Your Own Flesh

You are in a battle with your old nature. The flesh desires to do wrong. It has an appetite for evil. Even though you are saved, you still have that old, carnal nature. In Galatians 5:16, Paul said, *"This I say then, Walk in the Spirit, and ye shall not fulfill the lust of the flesh."*

Far too many Christian parents are allowing the flesh to win the battle, rather than walking in the Spirit and claiming the victory. There are three primary areas in which the flesh fights against us as we attempt to successfully parent our children.

Anger

"And, ye fathers, provoke not your children to wrath: but bring them up in the nurture and admonition of the Lord" (Ephesians 6:4).

There are many ways to provoke a child to anger. Being inconsistent and saying, "If you do that one more time," when you do not mean it, provokes anger. If you say something, follow through on it. They must know they can count on your word.

Your excessive anger provokes anger. Yelling and being mean is not effective parenting—it is childish behavior. There is a rash of anger on the part of parents, especially fathers, today. You are the spiritual authority and it is your job to keep the rules. However, you cannot do your job properly if you are acting in anger.

I was on a plane flying to preach at a conference not long ago. Sitting behind me was a man who was somewhat loud and arrogant in his speech. After we were in the air, he got the phone from the back of the seat in front of him and made a call. I heard him say, "Son, I told you this."

The boy's name was Joey. I do not know everything Joey was supposed to have done, but he had not done it. The man kept getting louder and louder as he talked to his son. Finally he said, "Joey, you are so stupid."

You should never say something like that to your children, no matter what they do or do not do. What do you think Joey thinks about himself? Let me assure you that Joey is going to look for the acceptance he is not receiving from his father from someone else. He may find it in a gang, a bottle, or in immorality. Your child needs acceptance instead of anger.

There is nothing wrong with reprimanding something done wrong. In fact, if you do not, you are failing to be a good parent. It is very wrong to degrade, belittle, and express anger toward your children. Do not demean your child in anger.

If you allow fleshly anger to govern your life, you are provoking your children and influencing them away from God, not toward Him. Children form their impressions of God from their parents, primarily their fathers. They need to see His Spirit displayed, not an angry, unjust spirit. That drives them away from both you and God.

Apathy

"And thou shalt teach them diligently unto thy children, and shalt talk of them when thou sittest in thine house, and when thou walkest by the way, and when thou liest down, and when thou risest up" (Deuteronomy 6:7).

The Hebrew word translated *diligently* is the word that also refers to the "sharpening of arrows." With their rather primitive tools, preparing weapons for battle required a great deal of effort.

Teaching our children requires an active involvement in every part of their lives.

Too many dads say, "Go ask your mom," rather than taking the leadership role God intends them to fulfill. An apathetic spirit has infected our churches and homes. We have allowed indifference to replace interest, and it is destroying Christian homes.

Parents who are not involved in their children's lives are failing them. Take time to teach your children. Many times we get tired and give up. Take your kids to church; do not send them. Families need to be together in church. Care enough to get involved and make a difference in the lives of your children.

Recently, a Christian seminary did a survey on parenting styles. They divided parents into four groups.

	High Control	High Control	
High Love	Authoritative	Authoritarian	Low Love
High Love	Permissive	Neglectful	Low Love
	Low Control	Low Control	

The neglectful parent tends to avoid his children. He would rather be doing almost anything else than being with them. Regardless of the excuses, this style of parenting leaves a child feeling unloved and abandoned.

The *permissive* parent allows the child to lead rather than leading him. He fears his own children. This is where apathetic parents most often fall. Their lack of concern leads them to allow bad behavior to continue.

The *authoritarian* parent pushes the child to conform rather than to mature. He has all the rules, but no relationship. He does not know the power of praise. He fails his children by not preparing them to do right on their own.

The *authoritative* parent fellowships with the child and leads him to maturity. He has a real relationship. In the context of fellowship and fun, you can say things and be heard, and deal with issues in a natural way.[10]

Care enough to get involved. Do not parent from fear. Children need to learn that there are rules and boundaries in life. Do not sit by and watch them do wrong. Know what is going on. Build the relationship. Explain the reasons for the rules.

Show your children that you care. The best way you can do that is to invest time in their lives. When I counsel, I tell people love is spelled T-I-M-E. You cannot win the battle if you are apathetic rather than involved.

Absenteeism

There was a time in this country when children could count on the physical presence of their parents. Dads came home from work every night, and normally moms were at home rather than being part of the work force. It is not a coincidence that the problems we see with immorality and juvenile crime today were very rare in those days.

Family life is challenging. The temptation is to focus on other things rather than the needs of your children. It is important to work hard to provide for the needs of your family. Do not feel guilty if you are working. That does not make you an absentee parent, but be fully involved at home when you are there. Take advantage of the time you have. Turn off the television and interact with your kids.

Make the most of every opportunity to do things together. If you try to do something once and it does not work out the way you planned, do not give up. Keep trying. Invest time and attention in the lives of your children.

---

[10] Gary Smalley, *The Key to Your Child's Heart,* (Tennessee: W Publishing Group, 1992)

Some days it may feel like nothing is working. Our culture is filled with pressures and attacks on the home. Sometimes the stress seems like too much to bear. I came across some comments recently that may describe the way you sometimes feel in your home.

> "Make yourself at home. Clean my kitchen!"
> "Who are these kids; and why are they calling me Mom?"
> "Don't bother me. I'm living happily ever after."
> "Is it time for your medication or mine?"
> "If I throw a stick will you leave?"
> "Therapy is expensive; popping bubble wrap is cheap. You choose."[11]

No matter how tough it gets, keep trying. Be actively involved with your children. Hockey great Wayne Gretsky said, "You miss 100 percent of the shots you don't take." Do whatever you can to make memories with your children.

Remember that the prodigal son wanted to go home. It was a place where he knew his father loved him. He turned his back on everything his father had taught him and went out into the world. When he finally came back to his senses, he did not have any doubt about where he wanted to be. He returned to his father's open arms. Make your house a place where your children know they are loved.

Fight the Corruption in Our Society

There is no question that our society is filled with sin. The answer to the corruption we see around us is not to withdraw into isolation. We cannot just set up a fortress and a moat and settle for reclusiveness. We must interact with the world. We must give our children the tools to survive outside the home.

I firmly believe in separation from the world and ungodliness, but this does not mean heading into the hills and living in a cabin.

---

[11] Lowell D. Streiker, *Nelson's Big Book of Laughter*, (Tennessee: Thomas Nelson Publishers, 2000)

We must be actively engaged and involved in fighting the good fight against that corruption.

Through Prayer

"If my people, which are called by my name, shall humble themselves, and pray, and seek my face, and turn from their wicked ways; then will I hear from heaven, and will forgive their sin, and will heal their land" (2 Chronicles 7:14).

We are not praying for America the way we should. We need to pray that America will have godly leaders in the White House and in Congress. We need to pray that our judges will follow the precepts of the Word of God and that the nation in which our children grow up will be one where God is revered and honored.

The great answer to our problems, as a society, lies not in the voting booth, but in the prayer closet. We have a responsibility to be fully engaged in society, and we will talk more about that in just a moment. My friend, Dr. Curtis Hutson, used to say, "There's more you can do after you pray, but there's nothing you can do until you pray."

We need to recognize the evil around us, cry out to God, and seek His face. We need to ask His forgiveness and His healing for our land. We need to be willing to be humble rather than proud. The good fight is fought on our knees.

If you want to fight for your children, establish a place of prayer. Make it a regular practice to pray for your children. Pray for their teachers, pastor, and future spouses. Pray that God will revive our nation.

Through Soulwinning

"Go ye therefore, and teach all nations, baptizing them in the name of the Father, and of the Son, and of the Holy Ghost: Teaching them to observe all things whatsoever I have commanded you: and,

lo, I am with you alway, even unto the end of the world. Amen" (Matthew 28:19–20).

Every Christian should be involved in sharing his faith. Do your neighbors know that you are a follower of Jesus Christ? Do your coworkers recognize that you are a believer? The power of salvation is the Gospel changing people from the inside out.

We cannot reform society from the outside in. The changes that need to come to our world must start with repentance in the heart. Taking the redemptive message of Jesus Christ to a lost and dying world is their only hope for true change.

Soulwinning is the most effective thing you can do to impact the world in which your children live. I am against pornography, abortion, drunkenness, and the homosexual agenda. But the best way to stop those things is not to picket the capitol or try to change the laws. The best way to fight is to be an effective witness of the life-changing power of the Gospel.

When people get saved, the Holy Spirit comes into their lives. He makes men and women new creatures in Christ (2 Corinthians 5:17). He changes how they view matters of morality and godly living. You should be sharing the Gospel every time you get the opportunity, and seek opportunities all the time.

Through Involvement in the Community

"Ye are the salt of the earth: but if the salt have lost his savour, wherewith shall it be salted? it is thenceforth good for nothing, but to be cast out, and to be trodden under foot of men. Ye are the light of the world. A city that is set on an hill cannot be hid. Neither do men light a candle, and put it under a bushel, but on a candlestick; and it giveth light unto all that are in the house. Let your light so shine before men, that they may see your good works, and glorify your Father which is in heaven" (Matthew 5:13–16).

I believe you have a responsibility to be registered to vote. Know what the issues are and where the candidates stand. Some strong believers need to run for office. If you get a venue in which you can shine the light further, do not turn the light down. If God gives you a platform, take advantage of it.

If God places you in a leadership position, stand for what is right while you are there. Even if it gets you kicked out, let it be known that there was a child of God present. The light is so needed in the darkness. Stand up and be counted. Be a visible Christian throughout the community in which you live.

Just as it was in Nehemiah's day, we are in the midst of a battle. The future of your children depends on your willingness to recognize and fight the battle for your children. Get involved in the lives of your children. Fight your own spiritual battles. Fight your own flesh. Fight the corruption in our society.

Take the tools that God has given you and build a wall of protection around your children. Do not allow anything to distract you from this vital task. Determine that, by God's power, you will do what it takes to succeed as a Christian parent.

Study Questions

1. Raising children is more about the _____ than about the _____.

2. List the three "F's" in fighting your own spiritual battles.

3. What are the four types of parenting styles?

4. In what three ways can you help fight corruption in our society?

5. Will your children change the world, or will the world change your children?

6. Do you allow anger to control your responses to your children? What do you need to work on in the area of anger?

7. When your children hear the word *home*, of what do they think?

8. Are you taking and making time to help dent our world with the Gospel through soulwinning? Do you have a scheduled time for soulwinning every week?

Memory Verse

1 Timothy 4:16—*"Take heed unto thyself, and unto the doctrine; continue in them: for in doing this thou shalt both save thyself, and them that hear thee."*

PART THREE

Precepts for Your Family

CHAPTER NINE

A Trio of Tools to Strengthen Your Family

Be not thou envious against evil men, neither desire to be with them. For their heart studieth destruction, and their lips talk of mischief. Through wisdom is an house builded; and by understanding it is established: And by knowledge shall the chambers be filled with all precious and pleasant riches.—Proverbs 24:1–4

There is nothing worse than buying something that does not work. Maybe you have had this experience with a television, radio, or toaster. You purchased it, got it home, plugged it in, and you found out it did not work.

A few years ago, a salesman came by our house. He said to me, "I have just what you need. This is a guaranteed spot remover. It will take up every spot in your house. It will clean every piece of carpet." Well, we have four children, so I bought that spot remover. We needed it.

I used it that night. I cleaned all the spots that were dirty. They went away, and I was happy. When I got up the next morning, I looked at the carpet. All the spots that I had cleaned had reappeared! I realized that the guaranteed spot remover was only good for 24 hours. I am glad that, when God gave us the Bible as a guidebook for our families, it is truly guaranteed.

Our relationship with God is supposed to impact every aspect of our lives, including our family lives. James 2:17–18 says, *"Even so faith, if it hath not works, is dead, being alone. Yea, a man may say, Thou hast faith, and I have works: shew me thy faith without thy works, and I will shew thee my faith by my works."*

James had such a tremendous confidence in the validity of his walk with God that he could say, "I'm not just going to talk about it. I'm going to show you my faith in God lived out each and every day." Our families can have that kind of confident, active, working, successful Christian walk, even in a world in which so many families crumble and collapse.

But some Christian families fail. Some do not survive the trials and challenges that attack every marriage. Does that show that God's plan is faulty? Is the Word of God faulty? No. When there is a failure, it is our practice that is faulty. The promises of God are always reliable.

When we come to the subject of applying Christianity, on a practical level, in the daily lives of our families, we need to remember that God has provided everything necessary for our faith to work. There are no missing parts. There are no missing ingredients that would keep us from having a family whose faith changes our lives—not just on Sundays at church, but throughout the week.

Everything we need is found in the Word of God. He has offered to provide us with the wisdom we need (James 1:5). I want to share with you three powerful tools that God gives us to build and strengthen our families.

The Guiding Presence of the Holy Spirit

The first tool for building a family with a practical, working Christianity is an understanding and yielding to the role of the

Holy Spirit in our lives. God gives us the guiding presence of His Holy Spirit at the moment we are saved.

What does it mean to be "born again"? People in our society use that phrase in many different ways. Romans 10:17 says, *"Faith cometh by hearing, and hearing by the Word of God."* So we see that no one becomes a Christian unless he first hears from God. At the same time that we are hearing the message of faith externally, there is also something happening internally.

This is the work of the Holy Spirit who draws men to Christ. This is why Jesus said in John 3:6–7, *"That which is born of the flesh is flesh; and that which is born of the Spirit is spirit. Marvel not that I said unto thee, Ye must be born again."* So the new birth is a spiritual birth. From the moment of that new birth, we have the Holy Spirit within.

The Indwelling of the Holy Spirit

In John 6:63, Jesus said, *"It is the spirit that quickeneth; the flesh profiteth nothing: the words that I speak unto you, they are spirit, and they are life."* It is the Holy Spirit of God who lives within every believer who quickens or brings life to the child of God.

The Holy Spirit's presence is vital for your marriage on a practical level. The humorist and poet Ogden Nash wrote:

> Just as I know that there are two Hagens, Walter and Copen, I know that marriage is a religious and legal alliance entered into by a man who can't sleep with the window shut and a woman who can't sleep with the window open.[12]

Marriage joins two people from different backgrounds. Not only are there major differences between men and women, but there are also major differences in family upbringing. One partner

---

[12] Ogden Nash, *The Pocket Book of Ogden Nash* (New York: Pocket Books, 1962) "I Do, I Will, I Have," page 21

was disciplined a certain way; the other was disciplined in an entirely different manner.

I think in nearly every marriage there is one spouse who rolls the toothpaste tediously from the bottom of the tube, while the other just grabs it and squeezes it in the middle. People from two totally different backgrounds come together in marriage and family life. There are conflicts inherent in these differences.

When these two very different people are indwelt by the same Holy Spirit of God, it is a wonderful thing. The Spirit of God is not divided. So in His filling, we can know true unity in our homes.

Every year the Rose Bowl is played not far from us in Pasadena. More than 100,000 people fill the stadium to watch the game. Of the 50,000 people who are cheering for each team, almost none of them will know each other, but they are unified around a common cause and purpose. Even if they are very different people, they can get along easily, because they are in agreement and harmony on an overriding idea—victory for their team!

In the same way that cheering for the same football team can unite people, the presence of the Holy Spirit will give unity to the life and relationship of two yielded Christians who are walking in the Word of God. As we adhere to guidelines and commandments of the Word of God, the Spirit of God works in our lives and helps us in our daily relationships.

The Holy Spirit's power from within is what holds the family together. The power to make our faith real on a daily basis is not our power, but God's power given to us at the moment of our salvation in the person of the Holy Spirit. God wants our faith to work in our families—in the family room, the living room, the bedroom, and the backyard.

The Purposes of the Holy Spirit

There are many purposes of the Holy Spirit's working here on earth. He convicts men of sin and draws them to God for salvation.

He works in our hearts and keeps us saved and secure in the family of God. There are three specific ways in which He works to bring success to our families that I want to bring to your attention.

HE IS OUR COMFORTER

In John 14, we have a record of the events that took place at the Last Supper. Jesus was preparing His disciples for the fact that He would soon be leaving them. In just a few hours, He would be crucified. Not long afterward, He would ascend up into Heaven and they would not see Him anymore.

In John 14:16, Jesus said, *"And I will pray the Father, and he shall give you another Comforter, that he may abide with you for ever."* One of the main reasons the Holy Spirit came was to be our Comforter. The word *comforter* means "one who comes alongside us and supports us in our times of need."

He is a comforter every day. Through the trials of life, we need a comforter. Sometimes misunderstandings come and feelings get hurt. The Spirit of God brings comfort to us if we are allowing Him to work in our lives.

I heard about a young couple who was preparing to celebrate their second anniversary. They were still in their "honeymoon phase." The husband wanted to make sure he did not forget his wife at that special time. He called up a florist and told them where his wife worked. He said, "I want to send her some flowers. On the card put 'Happy Anniversary—Year Number Two.' I want to let her know how much she means to me."

On their anniversary day, the flowers were delivered to the wife's office. When she opened up the card it said, "Happy Anniversary— *You're* Number Two." She sat there wondering about that and was not quite sure what her husband was trying to say.

When things do not go right, we need the comfort and encouragement of the Holy Spirit. He brings us comfort that no one else can bring. He brings us comfort when there is no one else to whom we can turn. We simply must learn to seek that comfort which He came to bring to us.

HE IS OUR TEACHER

John 14:26 says, *"But the Comforter, which is the Holy Ghost, whom the Father will send in my name, he shall teach you all things, and bring all things to your remembrance, whatsoever I have said unto you."* One of the most important distinctives of Baptists is the doctrine of the individual priesthood of the believer.

Every believer can go directly to the throne of grace. We do not need any mediator except for Christ Jesus. We do not pray through a man. What a blessing that is! All believers can study the Scripture for themselves. We can make decisions as the Spirit of God leads us.

I thank God for pastors, teachers, and evangelists, but every child of God has the privilege of opening his Bible and learning and understanding what it says, as the Holy Spirit teaches and guides him. When we need help knowing how to handle problems in our families, we can search the Scriptures and ask the Holy Spirit to show us what we need to do.

One of the most inspiring stories in American history is that of Helen Keller. Though both blind and deaf, she was able to overcome those handicaps and live a positive and successful life. That was due in large part to the dedication and devotion of a twenty-year-old teacher named Anne Sullivan, who devoted herself to Helen's education.

Anne taught Helen to read, write, and speak. She spent countless hours teaching a girl who was otherwise completely cut off from the world. Helen Keller went on to graduate from college, travel the world, and write twelve books, but none of that would have been possible without her teacher.

The natural man is totally blind and deaf to the things of God (2 Corinthians 2:14). They are completely beyond his ability to understand without someone to instruct and teach him.

The Holy Spirit takes the Word of God and uses it to teach us how to live. Of course, that requires that we take the time to learn and study the Bible. Many helpful books and materials are available on marriage, and I encourage you to take advantage of them. If you are a Christian, the greatest Teacher you can have to improve and strengthen your family lives in your heart.

HE GLORIFIES JESUS CHRIST

There is no way our homes and families can glorify Jesus apart from the Spirit of God. In John 16:13–14, Jesus said, *"Howbeit when he, the Spirit of truth, is come, he will guide you into all truth: for he shall not speak of himself; but whatsoever he shall hear, that shall he speak: and he will shew you things to come. He shall glorify me: for he shall receive of mine, and shall shew it unto you."*

God's purpose in every believer and Christian home is to receive glory and honor. The Spirit of God has assumed the task of bringing glory to Jesus as He works in and through our lives.

There are some people whose focus is solely on the Holy Spirit. This is an imbalance in their lives. They do not focus on glorifying Jesus, but that is what the Holy Spirit always does. When a family is Spirit-led, they make much of Jesus. They pray to Him. They want to learn of Him. They love Him with all of their hearts.

Years ago a visitor from the United States went to England. One of his friends there was a member of Charles Spurgeon's church. At the time, the Metropolitan Tabernacle had to hand out tickets for the services because of the large crowds who wanted to hear Spurgeon preach. Of course, the church member wanted his American friend to hear his pastor preach.

He made arrangements to make sure they would be able to attend a service. As they were leaving after the service, the American was asked what he thought of the service. "What a preacher!" he exclaimed. Unseen by either man, Spurgeon overheard the conversation and began to weep. When a friend asked what was wrong, he replied, "I wish he had said, 'What a Saviour.'"

Our families are not intended for our own honor and glory. Our purpose is not to call attention to ourselves. The achievements and accomplishments we gain should lift up Jesus, as we allow the Holy Spirit to help us bring glory to Him.

The Evidences of the Holy Spirit

How can we know that God's Spirit is helping us fulfill His purpose and mission for our lives? What are some diagnostic tests to show that we are on our way to becoming a family with a practical, working faith? Two clear marks tell us the Holy Spirit is at work in a family.

A GODLY LIFESTYLE

Such a family will have a different lifestyle than other families. What is that lifestyle? How is it described in Scripture? Galatians 5:22–23 says, *"But the fruit of the Spirit is love, joy, peace, longsuffering, gentleness, goodness, faith, meekness, temperance, against such there is no law."*

How many of us can say that those attributes are reflected in our families every day? How many of us would like those traits to consistently characterize our conversations? We cannot do that on our own. The flesh cannot produce those traits, but in the power of the Spirit we can enjoy those good attitudes toward each other. Walking in the Spirit is not an emotional experience reserved for worship services and detached from the realities of everyday life. It is the daily experience of the believer who feeds on the Word of God, prays, and obeys what the Bible says.

The fruit of the Spirit is something that should be growing in our lives every moment of every day. The true indicator that God is working is that we see this fruit coming forth day by day.

During our first week in Lancaster, I went to the bank. When I got to the window to make my deposit, I pulled out a Gospel tract and said, "I'm Paul Chappell. I'm the pastor at Lancaster Baptist. We're just getting started, and we'd love to have you come and visit with us."

The lady looked at me with fire in her eyes. She said, "I'd never go to a Baptist church. You do not believe in the Holy Spirit or tongues. You do not understand so many things about the Christian life." As that lady was saying those things in a very harsh way, I thought to myself, "Doesn't the Holy Spirit's ministry have something to do with love, joy, and peace?" She certainly did not show any of those traits in talking to me.

I do not want the kind of Christianity that gets all excited on Sunday morning at eleven o'clock but cannot help me love my wife on Monday morning at seven o'clock. The fruit of the Spirit is not only a Sunday thing. God wants our faith to work all the time, every day. We are to be godly—living like God—all the time as we walk in the Spirit.

A HOLY LIFESTYLE

Galatians 5:16 says, *"This I say then, Walk in the Spirit, and ye shall not fulfill the lust of the flesh."* The mark of the Holy Spirit is not an unusual emotional experience; it is consistent Christian character. Suppose a man comes home and tells his wife, "You don't look the way I want you to look. You didn't cook what I wanted you to cook. I'm tired of you." Is that a carnal, fleshly man or a Spirit-filled man?

That is a man walking in the flesh, following the old patterns of life. Someone who is walking in the Spirit will not fulfill the lusts and desires of the flesh. God gave us the presence of the Holy Spirit so our families would bring forth fruit that glorifies God.

When Tiger Woods turned pro, he signed a contract with Nike. He received $40,000,000 for wearing Nike apparel and using Nike golf balls for five years. When Tiger walks the golf course, he walks in Nike. It shows, outwardly, with whom he identifies. In the same way as we walk through the world, we are to walk in the Spirit.

Just as Tiger is clothed, identified, and walking "Nike," God wants us to walk in His Spirit so that we will not fulfill the appetites and desires of the flesh. Ephesians 5:18 says, *"And be not drunk with wine, wherein is excess; but be filled with the Spirit."* Drunkenness controls a person. It changes the way he walks and talks. It is a sad sight to see someone who is "under the influence" of alcohol.

In contrast to the way someone is negatively controlled by alcohol, God wants us to be positively controlled by His Spirit. If he walks in His Spirit, a husband will not treat his wife the way a fleshly man would. A wife will not respond to her husband in a fleshly way. Parents will not treat their children the way fleshly parents would. This is the practical result of living in the power of the indwelling Spirit of God.

A Biblical Perspective of Self

The second vital tool we must have is a biblical perspective of self. The world tells us that we have everything we need to succeed within ourselves. By the way, we eat that message up. It tells us what we want to hear, so we readily respond to it. Look at the incredible popularity of self-help books. Even in many Christian books, the emphasis is on self rather than on God.

Motivational and self-help speakers tell us to get up every morning and look at ourselves in the mirror and say, "Hey there, handsome. Go out there and conquer the world. You can do it because you are you." That is what the world says. The Bible says God has a very different perspective.

God's perspective is that, in ourselves, we are very weak, prone to failure, and, apart from His power, we cannot produce spiritual fruit. In our flesh we tend to fight against the Spirit's leading.

A wise Christian would look in the mirror and say, "You can't do a thing on your own. Lord, I need Your help. I need Your power." God is not impressed with our titles, positions, or accomplishments. He sees right to the core of what we are. Without Him, we will fail. We are naturally prone to walking in the flesh.

Galatians 5:17 says, *"For the flesh lusteth against the Spirit, and the Spirit against the flesh: and these are contrary the one to the other: so that ye cannot do the things that ye would."* We have a nature that is proud and selfish, producing devastating results if not yielded to the Holy Spirit.

Pride Is a Destroyer of Relationships

The flesh does not want to help with the dishes or give in when there is a disagreement. The flesh wants to get its own way. The flesh says, "I deserve to get what I want." The flesh is proud. It is the fruit of the Spirit that causes us to desire to do right, to live with our spouses and children with love, peace, and patience.

Pride is the destroyer of every relationship. Galatians 6:8–9 says, *"For he that soweth to his flesh shall of the flesh reap corruption; but he that soweth to the Spirit shall of the Spirit reap life everlasting. And let us not be weary in well doing: for in due season we shall reap, if we faint not."*

If we sow to the flesh—if we come home and speak evil to our wives and say words that are not kind to our children—in time, we will reap corruption. The family will be destroyed. We cannot expect to escape the consequences of pride and fleshly living. The Bible says that reaping what we have sown is a certainty (Galatians 6:7).

If a man sows to the flesh in lust, he is going to destroy his heart for God and his relationship with his wife. But if he sows to the Spirit in purity, he will reap life for himself and for his family. By sowing to the Spirit, we prepare to reap the harvest that God wants us to enjoy. Fleshly actions and fleshly speech are very evident in the life of someone who is not walking in the Spirit.

"And the tongue is a fire, a world of iniquity: so is the tongue among our members, that it defileth the whole body, and setteth on fire the course of nature; and it is set on fire of hell" (James 3:6).

A Spirit-filled Christian has a fresh vocabulary. I heard recently about a young lady in a youth group in another church. She got a job in a store in her town. She was doing well, and the manager asked her to make an announcement about a special in the cafeteria over the intercom.

She took the paper and the microphone and started the announcement. She thanked the shoppers for being there and described the special in the cafeteria. Then she said, "Once again we want to thank you for shopping with us today. Have a very nice day. In Jesus' name. Amen."

She was using the new vocabulary she had developed through her walk with the Lord. Pride destroys relationships, but seeing ourselves properly and allowing the Spirit to work will build up a relationship. It changes our attitudes toward ourselves and toward others. It changes our words and our behaviors.

Pride Is Defeated by Appropriating Scripture

We must understand that we cannot conquer pride through strength of will or determination. The power of God, found in His Word, is the only thing that can overcome our natural tendency toward pride. In Romans 6:6, Paul said, *"Knowing this, that our old man is crucified with him, that the body of sin might be destroyed, that henceforth we should not serve sin."*

Something wonderful happened at the cross. Not only was the payment for our sin made by the shedding of the blood of Jesus, but Jesus also conquered the power of the flesh. At the cross, Jesus provided victory for you and me that we might walk in the Spirit; but for it to take effect we must appropriate that power to our lives through applying and following Scripture.

We have a position of strength in and with Jesus. He not only died for sin; He also died unto sin. Romans 6:10 says, *"For in that he died, he died unto sin once: but in that he liveth, he liveth unto God."* Jesus broke the power of sin and put it out of commission. The old nature is still there; but in light of the cross it is rendered powerless. The old nature wants to continue fighting the battle, but it cannot win over a Christian who is walking in the power of the Spirit.

In Christ we died to all that belongs to the old life, and we are alive to all that is the new life. Because of His power, we are able to have a family with a faith that works. When we realize that our flesh is weak, we learn to ask the Lord to help us die to self. Paul said, *"I die daily"* (1 Corinthians 15:31). He, daily, reckoned himself dead to sin. He realized that only through the cross could he have God's strength and help.

A Daily Practice of Serving

The final tool we need to build a family with a real, practical Christianity is service to each other. A husband or wife who has the guiding presence of the Holy Spirit and a proper perspective of themselves will be led to a daily practice of serving one another. We will not serve our husbands, wives, or children if we are in the flesh.

The flesh does not want to serve. The flesh wants to stay on the couch and eat potato chips. The flesh does not want to get up and help the kids with their homework. The flesh does not want to go to church on Sunday night or read the Bible. The flesh wants to do what the flesh wants to do. If we are filled with God's Spirit, there will be a definite change in our homes. We will have a desire for different things. We will have a desire to serve one another.

Sometimes it is hard to have a servant's heart. I heard about what happened when a man got home from work recently. He fought his way through the commuter traffic, got into his neighborhood, and parked in his driveway. He walked to the front door and opened it up. He leaned up against the doorframe and said, "All right, Honey, I've had a rough day. Tell me again what everybody's names are." All of us have days like that.

Jesus gave us such a beautiful example of service when He washed the disciples' feet at the Last Supper. To fully appreciate what He was doing, you have to understand that washing feet was a disgusting and filthy job. In fact, under Jewish law, a Hebrew slave could not be commanded to wash a guest's feet. Yet Jesus, Lord and Creator of everything, volunteered for the task—washing the feet of His selfish and proud disciples.

Submitting to one Another

A daily practice of serving will manifest itself in two ways. First, we will submit one to another. Ephesians 5:21 says, *"Submitting yourselves one to another in the fear of God."* The Bible teaches that the husband is the head of the home, and Christ is the head of the husband. This verse is not talking about leadership roles, but about devoting ourselves to meeting each other's needs.

The wise husband says, "I'm going to submit myself to the meeting of my wife's needs as unto the Lord. I'm going to do whatever I can to meet her needs." The wise wife says, "I'm going to submit my own desires to the meeting of my husband's needs as unto the Lord." When both spouses are committed to this kind of relationship, the tensions that undermine so many marriages are eliminated.

There will be some things that one spouse wants to do that the other does not. Maybe she likes Chinese food and he does not. When the wife says, "Let's go have Chinese food," the fleshly husband says, "You always want Chinese food. I don't want Chinese. I don't like the taste." The husband that is walking in the Spirit will say, "Chinese food will be fine." (The intelligent husband will take her to the food court at the mall so she can have Chinese and he can have something he likes!)

He is submitting himself and his preferences to meet her needs. This is what Paul was talking about when he said we are to live *"preferring one another"* (Romans 12:10). It is making the choice to put the other person first. It is caring about what they want and need. It is a sacrificial love.

My wife enjoys going window-shopping. She likes to go out and mosey. That is not how I shop. When I shop, I determine exactly to which store I need to go. I determine exactly what I need. I go to the store, go to the proper aisle, and get what I need. I go to the cash register and pay for it. I go home.

Not my wife. When we go to buy something, we also go to see *everything* else, and we go to see *everyone* else. The fact is that I have to be prayed up and filled with the Spirit when she wants to shop. In my flesh, I will stand there saying, "Come on, come on, come on, come on. You already looked at that." (That is said under my breath, of course!) I just want to get through the shopping process. But submitting myself to fulfill her desires places our relationship on a much richer level.

Serving one Another

Second, a daily practice of serving is manifested when we willingly and cheerfully serve each other. If we are honest with ourselves, the real reason we do not like to serve is because we think it is beneath us. Again, it is important to realize that a servant's spirit will only come to those who are walking in the Spirit and who have a proper perspective of themselves. Only when we die to self are we truly free to serve others.

God is calling upon us to exhibit Christ-like, sacrificial love in the home. This goes against the grain of society. Perhaps you did not see this kind of servant love modeled by your parents. Perhaps you feel like your spouse is selfish and does not deserve to have his or her wishes honored.

It is a vicious cycle when both parties in the marriage are self-focused. Neither is willing to step forward and make the first move. So neither one gets to enjoy a marriage that works as God intended. Amazing things happen when we give up our rights and begin to focus on what we can do for our spouses.

I read this saying the other day. "An exhaustive study shows that no woman has ever shot her husband while he was doing the dishes." Following God's plan by serving each other in love works. It creates an atmosphere that builds up rather than destroys. It is a key building block of a happy, successful home.

It is only the Spirit-led Christian, with the proper perspective of self, who will serve in this way. Galatians 5:13 says, *"For, brethren, ye have been called unto liberty; only use not liberty for an occasion to the flesh, but by love serve one another."*

Some people take grace and liberty as an excuse to say, "You can't tell me what to do. I'm under grace." We hear this a lot in a church setting, as people debate standards and rules of behavior. But the same principle holds true in the home. Try telling that to your wife. Stand up for your rights and say, "I'm under grace and I'm going to do what I want to do." Obviously, that is not how you build a strong marriage.

God says that we are to use our liberty, not to do what we want, but to serve others. By love we serve. It is true that we are saved by grace and have freedom in Christ. But we are saved to serve—both God and others.

A few years ago we went to Sears and bought a treadmill. It is a very nice treadmill. You can press one button and climb a mountain without ever leaving home. You can press another button for a 20-minute workout. It has a panic button that stops it if you feel like you are about to collapse. You can put your palms on one of the bars, and it will measure your blood pressure and pulse. It has everything you could possibly want or need in a piece of exercise equipment.

However, since we got that treadmill I have not lost a pound. Not one. The reason is that I do not spend much time on the treadmill. It is a great treadmill. We can hang a lot of clothes on it. Every morning I get up and put my glasses on it while I am in the shower. But I have not lost any weight since we got it because I have not used it.

Is your relationship with God changing the way your family lives? You can do with your faith what most people do with their treadmills. Give it a try for a while; and then it will end up out on the curb in a garage sale.

Unfortunately, that is also what millions of families are doing with their Christian faith. They tried it for a while, joined a church, heard a sermon, went to a seminar...and eventually put it out for a garage sale. They decided the results were not living up to their expectations. Is that where your family's faith is headed?

The problem is not a failure of God's design. God is calling you to get on the treadmill and start going. Do the work that is required to achieve the results you want. Start learning to use these three tools drawn from God's Word. You have His unconditional guarantee that if you do, your family will be built up instead of destroyed. James said his faith worked on a practical level. It worked because it was real.

If you have the Spirit of God in your heart, you do not have to settle for walking in the flesh. Walk in the power of the Spirit. Ask God to show you how to respond, how to answer, and what to do in every situation. Take a look at yourself from God's perspective. See yourself as a needy person who cannot succeed in the Christian life without Divine power. Then begin to submit your needs and desires so you can serve your family in love. When you do, you will have a family with a real working relationship with God and each other.

Study Questions

1. When there is a failure, our _____ is faulty because God's _____ are always reliable.

2. Everything we ever need is found where?

3. What are the three purposes of the Holy Spirit?

4. List three powerful tools God has provided to build and strengthen your family.

5. When was the last time you allowed the Holy Spirit to comfort or teach you?

6. Is everything in life about YOU? Do your actions show this?

7. List several ways that you can daily practice the principle of submission.

8. When was the last time you consciously set aside your own preferences to serve your spouse or children?

Memory Verse

Romans 6:6—*"Knowing this, that our old man is crucified with him, that the body of sin might be destroyed, that henceforth we should not serve sin."*

CHAPTER TEN

The Priorities of a Spiritual Family

Likewise, ye wives, be in subjection to your own husbands; that, if any obey not the word, they also may without the word be won by the conversation of the wives; While they behold your chaste conversation coupled with fear. Whose adorning let it not be that outward adorning of plaiting the hair, and of wearing gold, or of putting on of apparel; But let it be the hidden man of the heart, in that which is not corruptible, even the ornament of a meek and quiet spirit, which is in the sight of God of great price. For after this manner in the old time the holy women also, who trusted in God, adorned themselves, being in subjection unto their own husbands: Even as Sara obeyed Abraham, calling him lord: whose daughters ye are, as long as ye do well, and are not afraid with any amazement. Likewise, ye husbands, dwell with them according to knowledge, giving honour unto the wife, as unto the weaker vessel, and as being heirs together of the grace of life; that your prayers be

> *not hindered. Finally, be ye all of one mind, having*
> *compassion one of another, love as brethren, be pitiful,*
> *be courteous:*—1 Peter 3:1–8

To understand the background of this epistle, you need to remember that Peter was writing to believers who lived under the tyrannical rule of the Roman emperor, Nero. Nero hated Christians. He authorized the persecution and execution of thousands of believers. It was a time of trial and testing. There was a great need for families to be the source of strength and encouragement.

We see the same environment today. Though Christians in America are not being killed for their faith, our culture still opposes everything that is right and good. You are not going to find much positive reinforcement from outside. Your family is supposed to be a spiritual oasis in a desert world that opposes God.

God's design is that your family will be a strong testimony for righteousness even as the culture around us collapses into darkness. To survive in this environment, your family must be a spiritual family—a family dedicated to following the leading of the Holy Spirit of God.

The fullness of the Spirit is essential for having a successful Christian home. In a home where the members are obeying God's command to be filled with the Spirit (Ephesians 5:18), there will be certain things that take priority and precedence.

Every priority that you have in your heart will eventually show in your life. The seeds that you sow will eventually produce a harvest. What we focus our time and attention on is what we will end up reaping.

I heard about a pastor who made a visit to a rather demanding church member. After she spent a great length of time complaining about all the things that were wrong in her life, he suggested they read a passage of Scripture for consolation. The woman rather piously told her daughter, "Honey, bring Mother the book she loves so much." The little girl quickly returned with the latest edition of the *TV Guide*.

You cannot hide your priorities for long. Those things that are important to you will eventually show up. It will be evident what really matters to you. So, as you attempt to build a spiritual family, here are some things that must be priorities in your life and home.

The Priority of a Godly Testimony

We need to return to seriousness in our Christian testimony. We must realize that people are watching and observing our lives each and every day. Therefore, we need to be constantly on guard so that we reflect a good representation of Jesus Christ.

"Likewise, ye wives, be in subjection to your own husbands; that, if any obey not the word, they also may without the word be won by the conversation of the wives; While they behold your chaste conversation coupled with fear" (1 Peter 3:1–2).

In the early church it was not uncommon for one partner in the marriage to be saved and the other unsaved. Peter is laying down a guideline for how those ladies with unsaved husbands were to behave in the home (and the same principle applies to men with unsaved wives).

God wants every one of us to be responsible for himself. I have heard it so often in counseling. "Well, I'll tell you what the problem is in our family. It's my wife." The focus is not to be on someone else, it is to be on you. How are you living? What is your testimony within the home?

If your spouse is not a believer, the way to win him to Christ is not by beating him over the head. It is by living a consistent Christian life before his eyes. This is what the word "conversation" means in this passage—it is our manner of living. What kind of testimony should a spiritual family strive to maintain in the home?

The Testimony of a Surrendered Will

"Submitting yourselves one to another in the fear of God" (Ephesians 5:21).

There are times in a spiritual marriage when a husband lays down his will to minister to his wife. There are times when a wife surrenders her preference for the sake of her husband. The principle is that your will is to be in submission, first to God, then to your spouse.

Having a surrendered will is a way to speak directly to your spouse's heart. That message is more powerful than words. This kind of spirit is a powerful testimony. Proverbs 15:1 says, *"A soft answer turneth away wrath: but grievous words stir up anger."*

Sometimes people think they need to nag and pester their family into doing things their way. That creates resentment. When you are trying to reach someone, the most effective way to see lasting change is to live a surrendered life. Your lifestyle is more powerful than any words you can use.

The Testimony of a Godly Lifestyle

"While they behold your chaste conversation coupled with fear" (1 Peter 3:2).

It is not a word that we commonly use today, but *chaste* simply means "pure and holy." The Bible tells us that a pure testimony is more powerful than a nagging, adversarial approach to a relationship. Many people live very different lives at home from the lives they lead in public. This is not pleasing to God.

Sometimes people say the Bible is old-fashioned and irrelevant. It reminds me of the story of an anthropologist who visited an island. He met a converted cannibal who was sitting outside his hut reading a Bible. The scientist said, "Don't you know that modern man has rejected that book?" The former cannibal replied, "Sir, if it were not for this book, you would be in my pot."

With the divorce rate at fifty percent, it is time we returned to following God's plan for our family. It is time we pay attention to what the Word of God tells us are the priorities for our families. The testimony of a pure lifestyle is powerful.

If you want to see someone's life change, let your life be the first one to change. Let your testimony be a witness to your family members who are watching you every day. Live a godly life within your home. Follow the commands and precepts of the Word of God in the way you treat your spouse and children.

"That ye put off concerning the former conversation the old man, which is corrupt according to the deceitful lusts; And be renewed in the spirit of your mind" (Ephesians 4:22–23).

In your family, you can choose to put on the old—the anger, harsh words, bitterness; or you can choose to put on the new—the Spirit of Christ. You can live like all your unsaved friends and relatives, even as a believer. If you make that choice, you will repeat their mistakes. Rather, we should let the Spirit of God flow through us and control our lives so that our testimony is pure and powerful.

The Priority of a Spiritual Heart

You cannot have a godly testimony unless your heart is tender for the Lord. What is on the inside will be reflected by your outward behavior. What is seen in your words and behavior is a manifestation of what is inside your heart.

"Whose adorning let it not be the outward adorning of plaiting the hair, and of wearing of gold, or of putting on of apparel; But let it be the hidden man of the heart, in that which is not corruptible, even the ornament of a meek and quiet spirit, which is in the sight of God of great price" (1 Peter 3:3–4).

Some people use this passage to say that women should not wear jewelry or makeup. I do not believe that is what God is trying to say. Instead, He is drawing a contrast between what is lasting and what is temporary and telling us to focus on what really matters.

Outward Beauty Is Temporary

In 2 Corinthians 4:16, Paul said, "...*but though our outward man perish, yet the inward man is renewed day by day.*" His point is not that we should not take care of our bodies. Your body is the temple of the Holy Spirit and should be treated as such.

But compared to the heart, the body is far less important. Our physical body is corruptible—one day it will die. Peter is saying that women did not need to be drawing attention to themselves by elaborate hairstyles, jewelry, and clothing. One of the trends of Peter's day in the Roman Empire was that women would pile their hair high on their heads and weave gold threads through it. He is saying that rather than drawing attention to ourselves, we need to grow and develop an inner heart for God.

God focuses on the heart. That is where He looks to evaluate us. The reason the heart is so important to God is that He knows what is in our hearts will eventually come out.

"*But the Lord said unto Samuel, Look not on his countenance, or on the height of his stature; because I have refused him: for the Lord seeth not as man seeth; for man looketh on the outward appearance, but the Lord looketh on the heart*" (1 Samuel 16:7).

There is a continual bombardment from our society to focus on the outward appearance. Books, magazines, and television all carry the message that how you look is the key to life. There are television shows devoted to nothing but "makeovers," complete with radical plastic surgery to give people a new appearance.

We need to recognize that appearance is a product of the heart, and we must focus first on the development of our inner man.

Inward Beauty Is Eternal

True beauty comes from within. Peter illustrates his point with the story of Sarah and Abraham. Over the years, I have heard preachers talk about Abraham's lie about his wife. Sometimes they make fun of Abraham for being afraid someone would want to steal his eighty-something wife. Yet she was still attractive, even at that age. Abimelech wanted her, and took her for his own (Genesis 20).

Why was Sarah attractive? Because the source of her beauty was found in her heart and her attitude toward her husband. Just like you put beautiful ornaments on a Christmas tree, the Bible says a meek and quiet spirit adds beauty to your life.

In Romans 7:22, Paul said, *"For I delight in the law of God after the inward man."* The heart is the totality of your innermost being. I grew up in churches where there was much preaching about how we should look. That is not a bad thing, as long as there are Bible principles being used rather than somebody's preferences. But sometimes we focus too much on the external. I once heard a thirty-five minute sermon against flared pants. I think God's people ought to look like God's people, but true holiness must begin with the heart. The purpose statement of our church says, in part, "to inspire people to develop a heart for God."

Guard your heart against the influences of the world. *"Keep thy heart with all diligence; for out of it are the issues of life"* (Proverbs 4:23). You must be cautious with what you allow to influence your thinking so that your spirit will not be drawn away from God.

In his book *Inside Out*, Dr. Larry Crabb said, "Outside cleanliness, whether the product of zeal or complacency, does not impress our Lord. With relentless penetration, He intends to deal with the filth we try to keep hidden beneath the surface."[13]

Conformity to the image of Christ can only be the result of spiritual maturity growing from the heart. That is why a pure heart is so valuable to God. Peter said the right spirit is *"of great price"* (1 Peter 3:4).

The Priority of a Respectful Manner

"Likewise, ye husbands, dwell with them according to knowledge, giving honour unto the wife, as unto the weaker vessel, and as being heirs together of the grace of life; that your prayers be not hindered. Finally, be ye all of one mind, having compassion one of another, love as brethren, be pitiful, be courteous: Not rendering evil for evil, or railing for railing: but contrariwise blessing; knowing that ye are thereunto called, that ye should inherit a blessing" (1 Peter 3:7–9).

We live in a disrespectful culture. Cutting and unkind words are commonplace. Some people take pride in their ability to be sharp with their tongues. In contrast, the Bible says you are to demonstrate honor and respect to your spouse. Honor means to esteem or value the other person.

No matter what else is going on inside the marriage, we should honor each other in light of the fact that we are "heirs together" as children of God. Your spouse was created by God according to His perfect plan and design. She is worthy of being treated with honor and respect.

If you have ever watched the *Antiques Roadshow* on television, you may have seen an old vase or lamp given a very high value. The key to the value of one of these items is the maker. When someone brings in a lamp stamped *Louis Comfort Tiffany*, you know the price tag is going to be high. Your spouse was designed and created by a far more skillful artist than *Tiffany* and deserves your respect.

God wants you to treat your family members with the same love and concern He has for them. Show them honor. They are of value to God, so they should be of value to you. Maintain good manners within your home. The home should be an island of sanctuary in a harsh world, not a place of put-downs.

---

[13] Dr. Larry Crabb, *Inside Out* (Pennsylvania: NavPress Publishing Group, 1998)

One of the wonderful things about the way God works with us is that He does not just tell us what to do, He also tells us how to do it. Here are five practical ways from 1 Peter 3:8–9 that will help you show honor to your spouse and children.

Compassion

Demonstrate the compassionate spirit of Jesus Christ to your family members. Compassion is defined as "sympathy or feeling for the suffering of others." Bible compassion is more than just a feeling. It is a feeling so strong that it produces a response and action.

"For we have not an high priest which cannot be touched with the feeling of our infirmities; but was in all points tempted like as we are, yet without sin" (Hebrews 4:15).

Jesus knows what our feelings are. He not only knows our needs, He did something about it. He left the glory and perfection of Heaven and gave up everything to come to earth and die for our sins. That is compassion.

God wants us to show active compassion toward our family members. Care about their needs and burdens. Share their joys and sorrows. Feel what they feel. Be actively involved showing compassion in your family.

Love

God expects us to demonstrate love toward each other. Your spouse desires to be loved, and to have that love expressed and shown. Your children need to know that they are held in your heart. When families are not characterized by love, they may give up hope for the relationship.

I believe there is always hope for your marriage and family, if you are willing to yield to the Holy Spirit. The fruit of the Spirit is love (Galatians 5:22), and the love He produces can face whatever tests come within your home.

In Colossians 3:19 Paul wrote, *"Husbands, love your wives, and be not bitter against them."* There will be tests to your love. It is important to face the reality that you will experience trials and difficulties in your home. Remember that Jesus' love for us never fails. Your love for your spouse and children should have that same level of commitment and determination.

Pity

Pity is demonstrating a tender heart. There needs to be a spirit of patience and forgiveness in your home. In fact, the key to an honoring relationship that builds closeness and unity is forgiveness.

"And be ye kind one to another, tenderhearted, forgiving one another, even as God for Christ's sake hath forgiven you" (Ephesians 4:32).

Let me tell you something about Paul Chappell. I did not deserve God's forgiveness. I only have it because of the blood of Jesus and His grace. Your spouse may not deserve forgiveness, but you can still give it to them because of what Jesus has done for you.

Do not be angry and bitter. When there are problems and disappointments, show pity and give grace to your family. We all need tenderheartedness and pity at times. Let go of your right to be angry. Replace those feelings with the same understanding spirit that you want extended to you when you fail.

Courtesy

Courtesy means to be lowly-minded, kind or friendly. It includes good manners, but goes beyond that to speak to our spirit toward each other, as well as to our behavior. Perhaps more than any other factor, the words that we speak reveal either our courtesy or our pride.

"Let all bitterness, and wrath, and anger, and clamour, and evil speaking, be put away from you, with all malice:" (Ephesians 4:31).

Treat the other members of your family, not as though you are better than they are, but as though they are part of the body of Christ and worthy of respect and kind treatment. Show them, through your words and actions, that you love and honor them.

It is also very important that you model courtesy and respect to your children and require it from them. Good manners begin at home. The breakdown of courteous behavior in our society can be traced directly to failures of parents to teach and expect it from their children.

Blessing

To bless means to honor, speak well of, or to celebrate with praises. Our words have tremendous power. You remember the childhood saying, "Sticks and stones may break my bones but words will never hurt me." It is a cute saying, but it is completely false. Your words can deeply wound the heart and spirit of your spouse or children, or your words can encourage, strengthen, and bless them.

Romans 12:14 says, *"Bless them which persecute you: bless, and curse not."* If you want to change the atmosphere and mood in your home, start blessing your spouse, even if he is upset and saying unkind things to you. It alters the relationship when your words build up instead of tear down.

You need to honor your spouse and your children verbally. Express what they mean to you. There should never be any doubt in their minds that you appreciate them. Find things that are worthy of praise and give them the blessing of your kind and encouraging words.

To have a family that succeeds, you must choose to place these things that are priorities with God at the top of your list. These three priorities of spiritual families are not issues of *can or can't.* They are issues of *will or won't.* With God's help you can have a spiritual family with a godly testimony, a spiritual heart, and a respectful manner.

On April 10, 1912, the *Titanic* sailed on her maiden voyage from England to America. People from around the world came to experience a trip on the "ship that couldn't sink." The ship was regarded as a marvel of technology and design. Those who embarked on that voyage had no feeling of danger.

Five days later 1,522 of them died in the icy waters of the North Atlantic. The tragedy is that those deaths were completely unnecessary. Days before the *Titanic* struck the iceberg, other ships warned the *Titanic* of the icebergs. They were ignored. One warning was not delivered to the captain because no one wanted to interrupt his dinner.

Rather than slowing down to give themselves a better opportunity to avoid the danger, they sped up to try to set a speed record for the crossing. While the *Titanic* was designed to hold 32 lifeboats, only 20 were placed on board so as not to mar the aesthetic beauty of the ship. The truth is that the *Titanic* was shipwrecked long before it hit the iceberg.

Your family is sailing in dangerous waters. The world around you is filled with dangers and enemies that are doing their best to shipwreck your family. Heed the warning. Make God's priorities your priorities. Have a spiritual family. Do what it takes to avoid a catastrophe.

Study Questions

1. What are the priorities of a spiritual family?

2. _____ beauty is temporary while _____ beauty is eternal.

3. Do manners really matter? What is some scriptural evidence?

4. Why should we show forgiveness and pity to others?

5. If you were asked to list your family's priorities, what would be at the top of that list?

6. If you are reading this book as a spouse with an unsaved partner, what is one way God would lead you to improve your testimony in reaching your spouse?

7. If God were to evaluate each member of your family today, would He find that the priority in each life is outward beauty, or is it inward beauty? What is the evidence?

8. On what manners does your family need to work, both practically and spiritually?

Memory Verse

1 Samuel 16:7—*"But the LORD said unto Samuel, Look not on his countenance, or on the height of his stature; because I have refused him: for the LORD seeth not as man seeth; for man looketh on the outward appearance, but the LORD looketh on the heart."*

CHAPTER ELEVEN

Portrait of a Loving Family

Submitting yourselves one to another in the fear of God. Wives, submit yourselves unto your own husbands, as unto the Lord. For the husband is the head of the wife, even as Christ is the head of the church: and he is the saviour of the body. Therefore as the church is subject unto Christ, so let the wives be to their own husbands in every thing. Husbands, love your wives, even as Christ also loved the church, and gave himself for it; That he might sanctify and cleanse it with the washing of water by the word, That he might present it to himself a glorious church, not having spot, or wrinkle, or any such thing; but that it should be holy and without blemish. So ought men to love their wives as their own bodies. He that loveth his wife loveth himself. For no man ever yet hated his own flesh; but nourisheth and cherisheth it, even as the Lord the church: For we are members of his body, of his flesh, and of his bones. For this cause shall a man leave his father and mother, and shall be

joined unto his wife, and they two shall be one flesh.
—Ephesians 5:21–31

Have you ever had the experience of getting a family portrait taken? I think that is one of the most stressful days of our family life! I do not know what it is about taking a picture of the whole family, but I would rather clean the garage or pull weeds! I would almost rather go to the dentist than go have a family portrait.

It seems to be even more stressful on ladies. Guys get up and comb what is left of their hair, look in the mirror and say, "You're ready to go." Ladies say, "Clear the bathrooms. We're going to need some extra time this morning." Finally, everybody gets in the car and you drive to the studio.

Invariably the wind will be blowing when you get out of the car. Now that is not much of a problem for me anymore, but there are members of my family who find that the wind negatively affects their hair. So there is another hair repair session once we get inside.

Then the photographer takes what feels like several hundred pictures. It is amazing to me that with all the choices you have to look through, you can never seem to find a perfect picture. There is always at least one thing that is not quite right. When the time comes, you pick the one that looks somewhat better than the others, and you are glad to have the ordeal over with.

The picture day experience can be a stressful day for your family. Your family also has a spiritual picture that God sees. His plan for your family is that it will be a picture of His grace. First Peter 3:7 tells us that the husband and wife are *"heirs together of the grace of life."* That grace is a gift from God that helps us overcome the stress and pressures of life.

Some people do not seem to find that grace. One man said to me, "Love is a dream, but marriage is the alarm clock." The Devil fights against families. He knows that if a family is succeeding in being a portrait of God's grace, it is a powerful testimony for Jesus

Christ. You need to be on guard, because Satan wants to destroy your family.

One of the primary sources of problems in the family today is selfishness. Paul told Timothy that in the last days, *"Men shall be lovers of their own selves"* (2 Timothy 3:2). Everyone comes into marriage with certain ideas and expectations. If you allow your focus to be on being served rather than serving, your marriage is in danger. Grace is what allows you to replace selfishness with a focus on what is best for your spouse.

I want you to look with me at a family portrait that reflects God's design for your marriage. Three basic components or elements make up what God considers to be a beautiful, loving family.

A Picture of Surrender

A successful marriage begins with partners who are willing to yield their wills for the good of the relationship. This is not common in many marriages today. Instead, we often find a free-for-all to see who can get their way first. God's plan for marriage is for there to be a mutual submission to each other.

Surrender to the Lord's Headship

"Submitting yourselves one to another in the fear of God" (Ephesians 5:21).

Nothing in your marriage will work according to God's design unless you are first of all surrendered to the will and plan of God. A loving family is a family where the fear of God controls decision making and personal interactions. God must be in first place in the home.

Submission is a voluntary surrender of your will to God. The concept of "submission" in this context is voluntarily retiring or withdrawing from the battle. The same word would be used to describe an army that lays down its weapons and stops fighting. A proper submission to God is the foundation for proper relationships within the home.

A wise Christian couple who wants a happy home must be willing to lay down their weapons—give up their tactics—and surrender to what God has for them. We need to be willing to give up our insistence on having things our way and surrender our lives to follow Christ.

"But he giveth more grace. Wherefore he saith, God resisteth the proud, but giveth grace unto the humble. Submit yourselves therefore to God. Resist the Devil, and he will flee from you" (James 4:6–7).

When two people are surrendered to God's will, they gain spiritual momentum in every area of their human relationship to do what is right. Someone is going to lead your home. My challenge to you is to make sure that that someone is the Lord Jesus Christ. Let Him be the head of your home.

Once when Mark Twain was on a lecture tour through the west, he stopped in Utah. While there, he had a long and rather heated debate with a Mormon on the subject of polygamy. Finally the Mormon asked, "Can you give me a single passage of Scripture that forbids polygamy?"

"Certainly," Twain replied, "no man can serve two masters."

There are some families in which the wives are in charge. There are some families in which the husbands are more than the head. They have appointed themselves dictators for life. Sometimes the children are the true leaders of the home. God's plan is for Jesus Christ to be the head of your home.

Surrender to the Lord's Design

"For the husband is the head of the wife, even as Christ is the head of the church: and he is the saviour of the body. Therefore as the church is subject unto Christ, so let the wives be to their own husbands in every thing. Husbands, love your wives, even as Christ also loved the church, and gave himself for it" (Ephesians 5:23–25).

God is the architect of the family. From the beginning, He set it up to run according to His plan. We must learn to surrender to the design that God has ordained for our families. God is a God of order and design. The Bible clearly teaches that He sets up structures and authorities to be obeyed in all areas of life.

Romans 13:1 says, *"Let every soul be subject unto the higher powers. For there is no power but of God: the powers that be are ordained of God."* God's plan is that "every soul" is to be under authority in his life.

The principle of obedience to authority goes against the grain of our culture. It is not politically correct to say that God has ordained the husband to be the leader within the home. Look around at the impact on families following what our culture thinks instead of what God thinks. The result is heartbreak, chaos, divorce, and broken homes.

God has a design for your home. You can choose to follow the culture, or you can choose to submit to God's plan. The major difference in the two plans is that, since God knows what He is doing, His plan works. Rather than trying to change God's plan, follow it in your home.

The fact that God has called the husband to be the leader of the home in no way says or implies that the wife is of any less value. One of the reasons so many Christian women react negatively to this teaching is that they have been indoctrinated by feminist thinking. Even within many churches, philosophy has replaced the clear teaching of Scripture on roles within the home.

God's distinction is made in matters of role and function so the family can operate according to His plan. God's plan does not mean the wife is inferior. There have been many times in my marriage when my wife had expertise in an area I did not have. I regularly seek her advice and counsel. In no way is she less of a person or a Christian than I am because she is a woman. I am grateful for a godly, spiritual wife.

In God's design for my family, I am responsible to make the final decisions and give direction to our home. I am thankful that my wife has allowed me to give that direction without having a rebellious spirit. She realizes that she is fulfilling God's design when she follows my leadership.

I heard about a husband who was taking his role as leader far too seriously. As a result, he was creating perpetual conflict in the home. Finally his wife said, "I've been praying for God to stop all this arguing by taking one of us to Heaven. And when He answers my prayer, I'm moving in with my sister!"

Godly leadership is patient, humble, and kind. A husband leading according to God's design is not bullying, demanding, or difficult. He has the courage to make decisions and stick to them. As you surrender to God's design for your family, there will come a unity as you move forward, growing closer to God and to each other.

A Picture of Security

"That he might sanctify and cleanse it with the washing of water by the word, That he might present it to himself a glorious church, not having spot, or wrinkle, or any such thing; but that it should be holy and without blemish" (Ephesians 5:26–28).

Jesus loves the church and has given us many wonderful things. One of the good things He gives is security. From the moment you were saved, you forever became a child of God. At that moment, you were sealed by the Holy Spirit. You can never be plucked out of the hand of God (John 10:28–29). You have complete security in Jesus Christ.

When I wake up in the morning, it is a blessing to know Heaven is my home. My eternal security is a settled issue. There is a wonderful peace in knowing that you have security. To have a successful, thriving family, you must establish that same sense of security in your home.

A loving family requires a sense of security to grow and flourish. Suppose you decided to plant a tree in your back yard. Every Saturday, you go out, dig it up, and move it to a new location. Will it grow and flourish? Not at all. Instead, it will wither and die. For love to grow and deepen, there must be a sense of stability and security in the relationship.

One of the most important things you can give your spouse and children is a stable life. They need to know they can count on you. I often tell people in counseling, "When you elevate dependability, you eliminate doubt." Be a person who keeps his word. Let your spouse and family know that they can always count on you.

Be accountable and dependable to your spouse. Build trust in your relationship. Trust is a very fragile thing. It can be easily lost, but it is hard to regain. So be careful to maintain the atmosphere of security in your home.

Through Protection

Every family needs to have protective boundaries around it. Christ's purpose for the church is that "he might sanctify and cleanse it." The word "sanctify" means to set apart. Just as the church is to be set apart from the sin and corruption of the world, your family needs to be set apart from the values of our culture.

Your family should be different from your neighbors' who are not believers. There should be things you do that they do not do. There should be things they do that you do not do. Your family should be protected from influences that are contrary to the Word of God. Your family portrait needs to reflect God's presence in your life.

SET APART TIME FOR RELATIONSHIP BUILDING

First Peter 3:7 says to *"dwell with them according to knowledge."* You have to be willing to invest in the relationship. The word "dwell" means to settle. There is simply no substitute for regular and extended periods of time together in developing a close family.

Get your PDA or your daily planner and put your family in a priority position on your schedule. Make appointments to spend time with your spouse and children. They need your time and attention. A feeling of security is built and developed through a knowledge of priority. How important does your spouse feel he or she is to you? Do your children know they are more important than your job or hobbies?

In the last century, a preacher named Clovis Chappell (no relation to me) wrote a number of good books. In one of those books he told the story of two paddleboats traveling down the Mississippi River from Memphis to New Orleans. For several days they traveled side by side. The sailors began to exchange remarks about the speed of their respective ships. Soon tempers began to flare and a race began.

As the race went on, the boats roared their way through the Deep South. Soon one of the boats began to lag behind. They had enough coal for the trip, but not enough for a race. Fuel was in short supply. As they fell further behind, one of the young sailors took some of the cargo from the hold of the ship and threw it into the furnace.

Once the sailors realized the cargo would fuel the ship as well as coal, they quickly caught up with their opponent. In fact, they reached New Orleans first and won the race. But they had burned all the cargo they were supposed to deliver.

Today there are men and women who have races they are eager to win. They want the promotion, the company car, the corner office. I have had some friends in the ministry who got so focused on things at church that they ended up losing their families. If we are not careful, we can lose sight of what is most important in our focus on the race.

God has given you precious cargo. Your spouse and children are more important than any job promotion or success. Your job is to see that your family reaches the destination intact. How many families fail because of the aggressiveness of a competitive captain?

MAKE GOD'S WORD YOUR AUTHORITY

In every situation and question that arises, there must be some standard for reaching a final decision. The best way to make good decisions is to have good input and counsel. There is no better source of counsel than the unfailing, unchanging Word of God.

Determine, ahead of time, that your family will follow what the Bible says. You cannot get too much of the Bible in your life or your family. Read it for yourself and with your children. Go to a solid, Bible-preaching and teaching church where you will hear the principles of the Bible explained and applied to your life.

"All scripture is given by inspiration of God, and is profitable for doctrine, for reproof, for correction, for instruction in righteousness: That the man of God may be perfect, throughly furnished unto all good works" (2 Timothy 3:16–17).

The Bible has the answers to the questions and challenges we face. Sometimes people tell me that the Bible is hard to understand. In my experience, the problem is usually not that we do not understand the Bible; but that we do not want to make the changes that obeying it would require.

In your commitment to follow the Bible, you will find safety and security for your family. God's Word offers you protection from sin and evil, but only as you obey it. One of the great tragedies I see in Christian homes is that people try to rationalize behavior they know is wrong. Decide, instead, that you will do what the Bible tells you to do.

If you give your child advanced knowledge of math and science but not of the Word of God, you have failed to equip him for life. I believe, strongly, in education, but the beginning of knowledge and wisdom is the fear of God (Proverbs 1:7; 9:10). The old saying reminds us, "Education without God makes men clever Devils."

AGREE ON THE BOUNDARIES

You and your spouse need to set up guidelines, on which you have agreed ahead of time, that your family will follow. I advise you to err on the side of caution. Romans 13:14 says, *"But put ye on the Lord Jesus Christ, and make not provision for the flesh, to fulfil the lusts thereof."*

In this verse, God is teaching us that we cannot afford to give the Devil even a small opportunity to work. In South Florida there is a combination park/zoo called Lion Country Safari. It bills itself as "the world's first cageless zoo." Visitors drive through large open areas, where animals from Africa roam freely.

One of the warnings they give you when you enter the lion area is not to crack your windows even an inch. Lions are so fast and strong that giving them even the slightest opening can result in disaster. Be on guard because the Devil is seeking opportunities to destroy your family (1 Peter 5:8).

Have rules for what you will watch on television. Psalm 101:3 says, *"I will set no wicked thing before mine eyes: I hate the work of them that turn aside; it shall not cleave to me."* Make up your mind and agree, together, that some things are off limits, and you will not allow them into your home. Know what your children are watching. If your children have a television set in their rooms, you are trading security for convenience.

Have rules to protect you on the Internet. Use a filtered service provider. Have guidelines that promote accountability. Communicate with your spouse so that there are no questions about what you are doing or where you are going to be. Set up boundaries to protect your home.

Through Cleansing

Our sins are forgiven when we are saved. The penalty for them was paid when Jesus died on the cross. Yet as we walk through a wicked world, we are contaminated by evil influences. This principle is illustrated for us by Jesus washing the feet of His disciples (John 13:4–10). There needs to be a cleansing within your family.

Sin is deadly. Rather than letting it linger, we need to identify and deal with it promptly. If your doctor told you that you had a small tumor on your lung, but he wanted to wait and see if it got any bigger before deciding whether or not to do anything about it, you would be looking for a new doctor. Sin is even more dangerous than cancer. Do not allow sin to remain without dealing with it.

The safety and security of your family depend on effectively responding to sin and removing it from your life. God has given us two primary tools to use in the cleansing process.

CLEANSING THROUGH THE WORD OF GOD

The Bible cleanses us in two ways. First, memorizing and meditating on Scripture keeps us from sin. Psalm 119:11 says, *"Thy word have I hid in mine heart, that I might not sin against thee."* Second, applying the Bible cleanses us when we do sin. In John 17:17, Jesus said, *"Sanctify them through thy truth: thy word is truth."* We need to let the Word of God cleanse our families as we teach and apply principles from Scripture.

CLEANSING THROUGH PRAYER

First John 1:9 says, *"If we confess our sins, he is faithful and just to forgive us our sins, and to cleanse us from all unrighteousness."* When we sin, we should be quick to seek God's face and His forgiveness through prayer. Jesus taught that confession was to be a part of our regular communication with God (Matthew 6:12).

Fulfilling God's desire and plan for your marriage requires that your home be secure. Security comes when we have set up boundaries of protection around our families and when we are seeking God's cleansing from sin on a regular basis.

A Picture of Salvation

"Husbands, love your wives, even as Christ also loved the church, and gave himself for it;" (Ephesians 5:25).

Your home cannot truly be what God means for it to be—a portrait of a loving family—unless you are part of His family. Salvation of the members of the family is the first prerequisite for having a Christian home. In this passage of Scripture from Ephesians 5, we see the plan of salvation illustrated for us.

JESUS PROVIDES SALVATION

No church, pastor, or priest can save you. Acts 4:12 says, *"Neither is there salvation in any other: for there is none other name under heaven given among men, whereby we must be saved."* Jesus is the only way to Heaven (John 14:6).

Jesus set an example and pattern that we can follow. Because of His great love, He took the initiative and came to bring us salvation. He made His love for us unmistakable.

There is no doubt about God's love for us. It was expressed over and over again. First John 4:10 says, *"Herein is love, not that we loved God, but that he loved us, and sent his Son to be the propitiation for our sins."* God's love for you is not based on anything you are or do.

The world's love is tied to a trait or characteristic. Love based on external things is never secure. If you love a person based on their appearance and they lose that positive characteristic, the love fades. God's love for you is eternal and unchanging. It is based on His nature, not yours. That is why Jesus came into the world to die for your sins—because He loves you.

JESUS PURCHASES SALVATION

Salvation is a gift. It is neither deserved nor earned. Romans 5:8 says, *"But God commendeth his love toward us, in that, while we were yet sinners, Christ died for us."* There was nothing good about us that made God want to save us. Yet Paul wrote that Christ "gave himself" for the church.

We sometimes say a person "gave himself" to a career with an employer. That is not what Ephesians 5:25 is talking about. It literally means Jesus Christ gave His whole life, suffering and dying on the cross for the sins of the entire world. Even though we were sinners and enemies of God, Jesus still came to save us.

Since Jesus was perfect and sinless, when He willingly laid down His life on the cross, His incorruptible, perfect blood became the payment for our sins. He died in your place and mine. He did that so that you and I could know Him and our families could be portraits of salvation.

We must simply accept His payment. How foolish it is to refuse that payment made freely, and insist rather on suffering the penalty of sin ourselves. The debt has already been paid. You and your family can enjoy God's free gift of salvation by accepting Jesus Christ as Saviour. This is the beginning of having a family that is a portrait of God's grace.

My wife and daughters love to make photo albums and scrapbooks. Their pictures, books, and supplies can cover the entire dining room table. They make pages for vacations we have taken, special events we have been to, and special people who are part of our lives.

It is a lot of fun to sit down and look through those books. They are filled with the memories our family has shared. As we look through them, I am reminded of the many ways God has worked in our lives. Maybe your family has photo albums like that, too.

In addition to those pictures, your family has a portrait that only God sees. If you were to show me a spiritual photo album of your family, could you show me a page for salvation? Do you have a page for surrender? Do you have a page for security? If your family is going to fulfill God's design and be a successful, loving family, you need to have all those pages in your book. Then you will be prepared to reflect His grace to the world.

Study Questions

1. What is the definition of submission?

2. What are three actions that provide protection in the home?

3. What are the two cleansing agents God has provided?

4. What Scripture passage illustrates God's plan of salvation?

5. Is your home in the proper headship order—Lord Jesus, husband, wife, children? Is everyone functioning God's way in his or her role?

6. Is your home a place of security, protection, safety, and comfort for each member?

7. Does your home have boundaries? Do you need to set any new boundaries? Are they set in love?

8. If we took a portrait of your family right now, how would you evaluate the results?

Memory Verse

Ephesians 5:23–25—*"For the husband is the head of the wife, even as Christ is the head of the church: and he is the saviour of the body. Therefore as the church is subject unto Christ, so let the wives be to their own husbands in every thing. Husbands, love your wives, even as Christ also loved the church, and gave himself for it;"*

CHAPTER TWELVE

The Hidden Enemy of the Home

> *Be ye angry, and sin not: let not the sun go down upon*
> *your wrath: Neither give place to the devil. Let him*
> *that stole steal no more: but rather let him labour,*
> *working with his hands the thing which is good, that*
> *he may have to give to him that needeth. Let no*
> *corrupt communication proceed out of your mouth,*
> *but that which is good to the use of edifying, that it*
> *may minister grace unto the hearers. And grieve not*
> *the holy Spirit of God, whereby ye are sealed unto*
> *the day of redemption. Let all bitterness, and wrath,*
> *and anger, and clamour, and evil speaking, be put*
> *away from you, with all malice: And be ye kind one*
> *to another, tenderhearted, forgiving one another,*
> *even as God for Christ's sake hath forgiven you.*
> —Ephesians 4:26–32

There can be no doubt that the family faces many enemies that are designed and empowered by Satan himself. He knows that the home is a picture of Christ and the church, and wants to destroy that picture. Every time a Christian family is broken, the testimony of Christ is harmed.

Perhaps the most effective tool in Satan's arsenal against the home is unresolved anger. Anger is destructive. Even worse, it is often unseen. That is why I call it the hidden enemy of the home. Something may be said or done that offends, and rather than dealing with it, the injured spouse will carry it around. Eventually those unresolved issues build into anger that can erode the foundations of the marriage.

It is not wrong to be angry. There are things that should stir us to anger. But it is never God's plan for us to be angry toward someone else. The proper exercise of anger is to be angry at a problem, but never at a person.

On the road to marital intimacy, there will be conflicts. The proper handling of those conflicts builds your confidence in each other and strengthens the marriage. The improper handling of conflicts breeds anger that undermines the marriage. The way you deal with conflicts makes all the difference.

Through studying the Word of God and many good books on marriage, I have identified six primary internal causes of conflict in marriage. Even though this chapter is about anger, you will notice that anger is not on this list. Anger is a by-product that develops when these causes of conflict are not properly dealt with.

The Six Primary Internal Causes of Conflict in Marriage

1. Immaturity

This problem is not restricted to just young people. Sometimes middle-aged people act very immaturely. This problem frequently arises for people who were not properly disciplined and trained as children. They never were restrained from self-will, so it carries over into marriage. Rather than react to problems as mature adults, they react as children would.

2. Self-Centeredness

If we do not appropriate God's grace, we will live totally for self rather than for our spouses. Marriage is not "all about you;" it is all about your spouse! A relationship based on self-centeredness is headed for problems.

3. Desire to Control

Some people spend their entire married lives trying to change their spouses. They never come to grips with the scriptural concept of becoming "one flesh." They fail to recognize that they are to be one in Christ; so they constantly struggle to make the other person conform to their ideas of what they should become.

4. Pettiness

You can spend your time fighting over little things like how to roll up the toothpaste tube or who did not close the door. My friend, Dr. Curtis Hutson, said, "Don't fight about things that don't matter." For some people nothing is too small to argue about. They focus intently on the tiniest details.

5. Pride

Proverbs 13:10 says, *"Only by pride cometh contention."* Anytime you have two people in a relationship who are constantly exhibiting a spirit of contention and conflict, you know pride is at work. Pride makes us unwilling to admit when we are wrong. Rather than apologizing, we attempt to defend our bad behavior.

6. Fear

When someone who has been hurt feels a conflict coming on, often he withdraws to avoid it, rather than resolving the issue. Frequently this is an attempt at self protection. Insecurity makes people unwilling to face problems. As a result of fear, problems are allowed to remain and fester rather than being dealt with.

One or more of these items are usually at the heart of disagreements within the marriage. If these root causes of conflict are allowed to remain without being addressed, anger will be the result.

We Must Refuse Anger

Too many believers are willing to accept anger as a justified reaction to conflict. We rationalize being angry by focusing on the offender instead of on self. We forget that God declares in His Word that we, as His children, are not to live with anger building up in our hearts.

Refuse to Harbor Anger

Ephesians 4:26 says, *"Be ye angry, and sin not: let not the sun go down upon your wrath."* We can be angry without sinning *if* we are angry at the proper things. We cannot be angry without sinning if we harbor anger toward others. Anger held within the heart is like an acid that eats the vessel that contains it.

Two kinds of people express anger. The first are what I call **pursuers**. They want to keep after the issue and bring it up again and again until they get to make their point and win the battle. The others are what I call **withdrawers**. They tend to pull back into a shell and hope things blow over.

Often people look at a couple and think the pursuer is the only angry one, but the withdrawer can be filled with a quiet anger that does not show on the surface. It is important to note that the amount of anger is the same in both cases; these are simply different ways to express it. Either person can harbor anger in his heart.

Refuse to Help Satan

Ephesians 4:27 says, *"Neither give place to the devil."* I do not believe there is one person reading this book whose desire is to help Satan. You *know* he is the enemy. Yet when we allow anger to dwell in our hearts, we are helping Satan by giving him room to work. You are giving him a place—literally inviting him into your life and home.

Our hearts are supposed to be filled with the Holy Spirit. There should be no room for the Devil. Harboring anger by allowing it to linger, unresolved, opens the door for him to come in and work against you and your marriage.

"To whom ye forgive any thing, I forgive also: for if I forgave any thing, to whom I forgave it, for your sakes forgave I it in the person of Christ; Lest Satan should get an advantage of us: for we are not ignorant of his devices" (2 Corinthians 2:10–11).

The Apostle Paul warned the church at Corinth that they could not afford to harbor any anger in their hearts, or else Satan would gain an advantage against them. If you harbor anger against your spouse, Satan has the advantage over you. Sam Ewing said, "It's wise to recognize that anger is just one letter short of danger."

Unresolved anger can fuel other sins. When a man harbors anger toward his wife, he may begin to justify immoral thoughts in his own mind. When a woman harbors bitterness toward her husband, she may begin to look outside the marriage to get her needs met.

When you go to bed with anger in your heart, you are sleeping with the enemy. The enemy is not your spouse—it is the Devil whom you have allowed and invited to come into your relationship. You are opening yourself up to his attacks.

Many couples attempt to deal with conflicts in ways that do not produce good results. Later on in this chapter, I will give you some tools that will help you resolve conflict; but first, I want you to be aware of common approaches couples use that are not effective.

Ten Ineffective Responses to Conflict in Marriage

1. Failure to acknowledge the problem

Denial is dangerous to your relationship. Proverbs 28:13 says, *"He that covereth his sins shall not prosper: but whoso confesseth and forsaketh them shall have mercy."* If there is anger in your marriage and you are not dealing with it, you are covering a sin.

Getting dressed up and putting on your church face every Sunday morning does not mean there is nothing wrong. Man looks on the outward appearance, but God looks on the heart (1 Samuel 16:7). Many couples refuse to admit there is a problem, but the only thing that accomplishes is that it allows anger more time to grow.

2. Withdrawal from real relationship development

Many couples come to the point where they decide intimacy and oneness are beyond reach. They have children, and maybe even grandchildren, and so they stay married, but they withdraw their spirit from the relationship, emotionally and spiritually.

They live in the same house, but settle for less than God means for marriage to be. Ephesians 4:25 says, *"Wherefore putting away lying, speak every man truth with his neighbor: for we are members one of another."* God wants truthfulness and transparency in relationships. Some people withdraw because they have simply given up.

3. Ignoring the significance of the conflict

The temptation is to say, "Well, everybody has a certain level of anger. I can handle it." That attitude accepts the danger and damage of anger, and allows it to remain unchecked and unresolved. While there are minor issues, there are no minor conflicts.

Each one is an indication of a problem that needs to be identified and addressed. Solomon warned about the danger of "the little foxes" (Song of Solomon 2:15). When you are tempted to ignore an issue because it seems too small for concern, you are missing an opportunity to resolve a conflict before it becomes a major issue.

4. Spiritualizing the problem

Sometimes a spouse in counseling will say, "Well, the Devil's just fighting us." That may be true, but saying it does not do anything to solve the problem. Spiritual "happy-talk" does not change the reality of a problem that needs to be addressed.

We need to take responsibility for resolving conflicts in our marriages. We need to be alert to attacks from the Devil, but realize that he may be attacking us because, through anger, we have given him the opening he is using against us (Ephesians 4:27).

5. "Gunny Sacking"

I have heard so many things in counseling over the years. "You would not believe what she did on August 12, 1972." "You wouldn't believe what he said on November 18, 1981 at 3:00." These people are harboring bitterness in their hearts. They are keeping their hurts in "gunnysacks" and dumping them out at their will. No good effect can possibly come from that.

Once a matter has been addressed, and forgiveness is sought and received, it should never come up again. That is the way God deals with our sins. He said, *"I, even I am he that blotteth out thy transgressions for mine own sake, and will not remember thy sins"* (Isaiah 43:25). No one wins when you keep score against your spouse.

6. Attacking the person instead of the problem

This is a carnal tactic. This is what the world does. Attacking each other does not do anything to bring about a solution. This makes things personal and hurtful. Personal attacks are sinful. Part of being angry without sinning is directing that anger toward the problem instead of toward the person.

You have a gift from God in the person of your spouse. Attacking the person you married devalues God's gift and undermines your relationship. If there is a legitimate issue of conflict, seek the causes rather than turning your arguments against your spouse.

7. Blaming someone else

This is not a new tactic. Adam blamed the very first sin in the Garden of Eden on Eve. She turned around and blamed the serpent (Genesis 3:9–13). It is part of our fallen human nature to pass the buck. We often try to avoid responsibility for our words and actions.

"I'm the way I am because I'm married to her." "I do these things because of the stress he puts me under." I frequently hear couples say things like this in counseling, but conflict cannot be resolved until personal responsibility is accepted. Instead of blaming your spouse, look at what you have done to contribute to the problem.

8. Desiring to win at any cost

There are some arguments that are better lost. Nobody ever really wins. You may think that you have won a battle, but you really just robbed a piece of your spouse's heart that you can never give back. In the heat of the moment, harsh words can be spoken that will echo for years to come.

After the First World War, Britain and France demanded that Germany pay enormous sums of money as reparations for the war. That financial strain contributed to the collapse of the German economy and the rise of Adolph Hitler to power. The Allies "won," but the long-term costs were incredibly high. Your relationship is far more important than who wins any one particular argument.

9. Giving in to avoid conflict

If you are "giving in" because the Holy Spirit is convicting you, this is the right thing to do. But "giving in" is often "wimping out" rather than having the courage to speak the truth. Someone once said, "Sometimes silence is golden; but it can also be plain yellow."

"Don't rock the boat" is the governing philosophy in some marriages. It is important that you be willing to address the issues. I am not saying you should be stubborn or insist on a fight for the sake of having a fight. What I am saying is do not give in simply to avoid the conflict.

10. Buying a gift

Most of these techniques are used equally, but this one seems to be the special province of men. The picture of a man bringing home a dozen roses to get himself out of the doghouse is familiar to us all, but you cannot buy your way out of dealing with a conflict.

Proverbs 15:16 says, *"Better is little with fear of the Lord than great treasure and trouble therewith."* All the gifts in the world will not make up for an unresolved issue. You must make a commitment to dealing with the cause of the conflict rather than relying on gifts to do the talking for you.

Learn to watch out for these ineffective techniques. If you find you are using one of them, stop and find a way to settle the conflict rather than sweeping it under the rug. You are not refusing anger if you do not deal with it. Instead, you are allowing the Devil room to work in your life.

We Must Resolve Anger

There is no way to avoid anger; but there are ways to deal with it effectively and resolve it according to the principles of God's Word. Since anger is a hidden enemy of your home, you need to constantly be on guard to be sure it is not working undetected to undermine your relationship.

Guard Your Heart

Ephesians 4:30 says, *"And grieve not the holy Spirit of God, whereby ye are sealed unto the day of redemption."* The Holy Spirit is the one Person of the Trinity who takes up residence in your life the day you are saved. He is the sealing presence and Person of God living in you.

The word *grieve* means "to afflict with sorrow." I want you think about this. When I have sin in my heart, when I harbor anger in my heart, I afflict the Holy Spirit with sorrow. Anger left unresolved grieves the Holy Spirit.

Anger harbored toward someone else limits the work of the Holy Spirit in your own life. This is a very dangerous thing. When there is anger, you cannot feel the Holy Spirit's conviction. That is why Christians who are not guarding their hearts against anger can do very destructive things. They are quenching the Holy Spirit and not sensing His convicting power. They can go to great depths in the damage they do to their spouses. I have seen many Christian homes destroyed because someone was controlled by anger rather than by the Holy Spirit.

When we talk about quenching a fire, most of us imagine pouring water on it. When you go camping, one of the first things you learn is the importance of completely putting out the fire. You do not want to leave even a spark that might bring the fire back to life. So you thoroughly drench it.

When you harbor anger toward your spouse in your heart, you are pouring water on the fire of the Holy Spirit. Just like wet wood does not burn well, anger keeps you from responding to the prompting and conviction of the Holy Spirit. You need to guard your heart against anger so He can work within you.

Guard Your Mouth

Ephesians 4:29 says, *"Let no corrupt communication proceed out of your mouth, but that which is good to the use of edifying, that it may minister grace unto the hearers."* The word *corrupt* means "bad, decayed, filthy, or defiled." When you use harsh or angry words with your spouse, you are hurting the heart of your relationship.

First Corinthians 15:33 says, *"Be not deceived: evil communications corrupt good manners."* The word *manners* is talking about our relationships. Harsh words ruin good relationships. Resolving anger requires that we guard our mouths. The pain of uncontrolled, angry words lingers long after the original argument is over.

"...Out of the abundance of the heart the mouth speaketh" (Matthew 12:34). The reason angry words come out in the heat of an argument is that there are angry thoughts being harbored in the heart. You cannot resolve anger unless you deal with the conflicts that cause it.

Seven Steps to Resolving Conflict

1. Keep your heart for God.

Proverbs 4:23 says, *"Keep thy heart with all diligence; for out of it are the issues of life."* Changing your spouse is not the first step to resolving conflicts! The first step is to seek God and develop a sensitive heart to Him.

Do not allow pride or stubbornness! Do not insist on having your way or winning an argument! Be tender to the leading of the Holy Spirit when He prompts you to make things right. One of the great secrets of successful Christian couples is that they have hearts that are tender and responsive to God.

2. Bear with your spouse's weaknesses.

Your spouse has weaknesses! Your spouse's spouse does, too! No marriage is perfect because no marriage is made of perfect people. Romans 15:1 says, *"We then that are strong ought to bear the infirmities of the weak, and not to please ourselves."*

Be spiritual enough to bear the weaknesses of your spouse. Do not begrudge those weaknesses. Instead, work with him to develop strengths in areas where he is lacking. The Devil deceives many people into thinking they can find someone better than their current spouses, but that is always a lie. Do not expect your spouse to be perfect.

3. Seek God's knowledge.

Proverbs 24:3 says, *"Through wisdom is an house builded; and by understanding it is established."* We always have more to learn. Too many people reach a point when they stop learning and growing, both as believers and in their marriages.

Take the time to learn the principles of God's Word that apply to your marriage. He designed marriage, and He knows how it can be successful. Read and study Bible-based books about marriage. As you learn and follow God's principles, your relationship with your spouse will be transformed by God's grace.

4. Spend time praying together.

There is much truth in the old cliché that says, "The family that prays together stays together." It is hard to argue with your spouse if you have just been spending time in prayer together. It brings your hearts together when you both go before God in prayer.

Few things will strengthen your faith in God and your relationship more than seeing answers to your prayers together. Make it a practice in your marriage to spend time praying together about specific needs. Rejoice together at the answers you receive. It will draw your hearts toward each other and away from problems you might be facing.

5. Seek godly counsel.

If you reach a point of impasse where you are dealing with issues that you cannot resolve, find someone who can help. I want to caution you very strongly *never* to seek counsel from the world. Find someone who bases his advice about your situation on the Word of God (Psalm 1:1–3).

It is not a sign of failure or weakness to seek counsel. Proverbs 13:18 says, *"Poverty and shame shall be to him that refuseth instruction: but he that regardeth reproof shall be honoured."* Over the years at our church, there have been many marriages saved because the partners were willing to seek and heed advice from godly men and women who knew how to help them.

6. Keep a clean slate.

Resolve issues quickly. Do not let things linger or fester. Paul taught this principle when he said, *"Let not the sun go down upon your wrath"* (Ephesians 4:26). You should never allow an issue to remain unresolved, even through the night.

Once you have resolved an issue, do not go back to it. Never bring it up again. It is very destructive to your relationship to reopen old wounds. Let God fully heal those wounds. Do not bring up past faults and failings. Do not dwell on these things in your mind. Let the past stay in the past.

7. Accentuate the positive.

I am not referring to the power of positive thinking. I am saying that your attitude toward your spouse is largely a question of focus. You can always look at the negative things, but why not look at the good, positive, and beautiful things?

Do not focus on the problems. No matter where your marriage is today, there are good things you can find to think on and praise in your spouse. If that is where your focus is, the problems will not seem so large and overwhelming. You always have the choice to concentrate on what is right rather than on what is wrong.

It is more rewarding to *resolve* a conflict than to *dissolve* a relationship. The point of dealing with a conflict is not to place the blame, but rather to fix the problem. Following these seven practical steps to resolve conflicts can help you guard your heart and home against the hidden enemy of anger.

We Must Replace Anger

Our emotions do not exist in a vacuum. We cannot simply *remove* anger; we must also *replace* it with spiritual characteristics that protect us against anger's destruction. God wants us to have proper attitudes toward our spouses rather than angry spirits.

Replace Anger with Humility

Anger and the contention it breeds are based in pride. When we have too high an opinion of ourselves, we are not willing to listen to the views of others or consider that we might be in the wrong. As we humble ourselves, we open up the possibility of resolving conflict.

"Let all bitterness, and wrath, and anger, and clamour, and evil speaking, be put away from you, with all malice: And be ye kind one to another, tenderhearted, forgiving one another, even as God for Christ's sake hath forgiven you" (Ephesians 4:31–32).

Be tenderhearted. Be willing to recognize and confess when you are the one who is in the wrong. Do not be proud and stubborn. Seek the forgiveness of your spouse when you cause offense. Since these are not natural human traits, realize that you will need to be sensitive to the promptings of the Holy Spirit to exhibit humility in your marriage.

God is able to break proud people (Daniel 4:37). It is far better if we humble ourselves before Him (1 Peter 5:6). If you are not humble toward your spouse, you will not admit you are wrong, even if you know it. You will try to hang on and defend yourself. This only leads to a cycle of escalating conflict that eats away at your marriage.

Replace Anger with Forgiveness

Are you living with unresolved conflict? You can choose to forgive. If God can forgive us, we can forgive each other. Colossians 3:13 says, *"Forbearing one another, and forgiving one another, if any man have a quarrel against any: even as Christ forgave you, so also do ye."*

The principle here is that we should forgive others in the same way Christ forgave us. He does not insist on our proving we really mean it. He places no conditions on His forgiveness. He forgives fully and freely as soon as we ask Him to. He never withholds forgiveness because our offense is too big. His forgiveness is the pattern we are to follow in our relationships.

In fact, if we want God to forgive us, we must forgive each other. Jesus taught His disciples how to pray. *"And forgive us our debts, as we forgive our debtors"* (Matthew 6:12). Do you want God to forgive you the way you forgive your spouse? We need to trade the bitterness of anger for the grace of forgiveness.

Years ago, when our church was still meeting in our old building, I drove to the office one day. When I pulled into the parking lot, my tire sank into the asphalt all the way to the axle. After doing some investigating and a little digging, we found there was a huge hole under the parking lot. It was filled with water.

What we discovered was that the water main had a leak. It was obviously an old pipe. It was rusty and corroded. The pipe was not ruptured; in fact, the leak was quite small. It looked almost like a squirt gun shooting out water. But that pipe had been leaking for so long that it created a sinkhole ten feet wide and four feet deep.

I learned, that day, that just a little leak can create a big problem over time. Anger, left unresolved in your marriage, will have the same effect. Deal with it. Do not allow it to destroy the foundations of your home. So many times when a relationship collapses, it is not because of a sudden event. It is simply the cumulative effect of years of hidden damage underneath the surface.

The hidden enemy of your family is anger. If there is something in your heart that you are holding against your spouse, deal with it today. This is one of the most important things you can do to guard the foundations of your marriage and preserve your family as a reflection of the love of Jesus Christ.

Study Questions

1.   What is Satan's most effective tool against the home?

2.   What are the six primary internal causes of conflict in marriage?

3.   List the ten ineffective responses to conflict. Are you practicing any of them?

4.   List the seven steps of resolving conflict.

5.   How could you apply these seven steps to a conflict you are facing right now?

6.   Are you a pursuer or a withdrawer?

7.   What two qualities replace anger?

8.   Are you holding anything in your heart against your spouse right now?

Memory Verse

Ephesians 4:30—*"And grieve not the holy Spirit of God, whereby ye are sealed unto the day of redemption."*

CHAPTER THIRTEEN

Leaving a Godly Legacy

Children, obey your parents in the Lord: for this is right. Honour thy father and mother; which is the first commandment with promise; That it may be well with thee, and thou mayest live long on the earth. And, ye fathers, provoke not your children to wrath: but bring them up in the nurture and admonition of the Lord.—Ephesians 6:1–4

The attitude a society has toward children tells you much about that society's values and belief system. Unfortunately, we live in a world where children are often viewed as a commodity or, even worse, an inconvenience.

I recently read a news report that parents have now gone beyond just wanting to find out whether they are having a boy or girl. Now some parents are seeking doctors to help them choose the gender before the child's conception. Instead of being content with a boy or girl as God chooses, parents want that to be their choice. They are seeking help from doctors who are trying to play God.

Even more revealing about our attitudes toward children is the widespread prevalence of abortion. In many countries like

India and China, millions of girls are being aborted because their parents want to have boys. Any time the life of a beating heart in the womb of a mother is taken, it is murder.

We live in a day in which children are considered optional. Many people view children as a hassle, as unwanted items in their families. The Bible says just the opposite. Psalm 127:3 says, *"children are an heritage of the Lord...."* The word *heritage* means "a possession or an inheritance." In other words, your children are precious gifts from God and you should view them as such.

We have an opportunity and a responsibility to rear them to follow and love God with all their hearts. In this final chapter, we will explore how to leave a godly heritage of faith to the next generation.

You see, our job as parents is not done until we have passed on our faith to our children and have prepared them to do the same with their children. Dr. Ed Johnson, who pastored for years in Minnesota, said, "You don't know whether you've truly succeeded as parents until you see how your grandchildren turn out." I believe he is right.

This kind of legacy of faith spans generations, but it will not develop by default. You could leave your children a million dollars. You could leave them possessions—stocks, bonds, or real estate. But if you do not leave them a godly example, if you do not cultivate in their hearts a love for the Lord, if you do not prepare them to succeed as Christian parents, then you have not given them what matters most in this life!

How can we leave a godly heritage to those who follow us? How can we know that all those who come behind us will find us faithful?

Model the Christian Life Before Our Children

The greatest gift you can give is a good example. More than anything else, I want my children to be able to look back and say, "I had a mother and father who were faithful to God. They modeled the Christian life before me."

Seeing a successful role model has a tremendous impact on people! Back in the early 1950s, it was widely accepted that it was impossible for a human being to run a mile in less than four minutes. Hundreds of the best athletes in the world had tried and failed. But a runner named Roger Bannister, from Harrow, England, refused to listen.

When he completed a one mile race in 3 minutes 59.4 seconds in May of 1954, it had a startling impact. In the next few months, more than a dozen other runners also succeeded in breaking the four-minute barrier. Knowing that someone else had succeeded gave the runners the confidence that they, too, could do it.

The truth is, our children are growing up in a world in which they can easily be discouraged about the possibility of succeeding in the Christian family. But we have the opportunity to give to our children a model of a working Christian family.

Model the Christian Life in Our Daily Walk

Proverbs 23:26 says, *"My son, give me thine heart, and let thine eyes observe my ways."* The fact is that children do what children see. When I was in the third grade, I had a friend named Billy Blocker. Billy was a tall kid with blonde hair and lots of freckles. He was my football playing buddy. We would put on little plastic football helmets we got for Christmas and go out to play football in the yard.

There are certain things you remember from childhood that are clearly imprinted on your memory. Billy's father was the only person I knew who smoked. It always looked funny to me, since I had not been raised around it. I had lots of questions. How can smoke come out of a person's nose and mouth at the same time? Does it come out their ears? I watched to see.

Billy's dad was a chain smoker. Sometimes he would stand by the field, watching us play. He would smoke the entire time. I remember hearing him say, "Billy, whatever you do, don't smoke these nasty things. These are awful. They're terrible for your health." It really did not surprise me when one day I walked behind the school and found Billy smoking a cigarette. Children do what children see.

What do your children see in your life? Ephesians 6:4 says, "*...Ye fathers, provoke not your children to wrath....*" Few things generate disappointment and rebellion in the heart of a child like an inconsistent model of the Christian life. Teenagers are experts at finding inconsistencies and putting a two-by-four through them.

Our goal must be to show a consistent model. The word *provoke* used in Ephesians 6:4 means "to exasperate to anger." There are many young people living with anger today. Earlier we talked about the large number of men in prison who were raised in a home without a father. This environment breeds anger. Most of those men never saw a successful model after which they could pattern themselves.

Many times, as parents, we send forth rejection in the tone of our voices or in the way we administer discipline. There should never be anger or rejection in discipline. I heard about a mother who had fallen into the habit of yelling and screaming at her children. She felt that was the only way to get their attention.

She came down with laryngitis and was unable to speak above a whisper for a week. At the end of the week she told a friend, "I found my children were far more well-behaved. They were much better natured when I could only speak to them in a whisper instead of shouting at them."

Maintaining order and discipline in your family has nothing to do with the tone or volume of your voice; it has everything to do with the character of your heart and the commitment of your life. We are to model the Christian life in our daily walk.

Model the Christian Life in Our Marriage

The husband-wife relationship is a picture of God's love for the church. The church is called the bride of Christ. The picture of love that our children see in our marriages is the picture they will have of God's love! It is a reflection of what the love of God really means on a practical level.

"And Adam said, This is now bone of my bones, and flesh of my flesh: she shall be called Woman, because she was taken out of Man. Therefore shall a man leave his father and his mother, and shall cleave unto his wife: and they shall be one flesh" (Genesis 2:23–24).

The greatest gift a father can give his children is to love their mother. Children receive a great sense of security by seeing love demonstrated between their parents. Conversely, they receive a great sense of insecurity when they see fighting and hear talk of divorce. This insecurity plagues and haunts young people for years to come. It will impact their own families down the road.

That is why the Bible says in Ephesians 5:25, *"Husbands, love your wives, even as Christ also loved the church, and gave himself for it."* We must learn how to keep our family commitments. We must learn how to keep our promises. We may live in an age in which divorce is common, but we do not have to give up or give in.

In this day and age, because of the constant fighting between husbands and wives, too many people decide to just give up and get a divorce. As a result, children are not seeing a consistent, loving model. This breeds insecurity within their hearts. It causes them to question the marital relationship and whether it is possible for a marriage to succeed at all!

I believe this is one of the reasons the age at which people get married is going up in the United States. They have lost confidence that marriage can work. We must provide our children with an example of a marriage relationship that works as God intended.

Mentor our Children in the Christian Life

Modeling is primarily the display of a godly testimony. Mentoring refers to a parent who is actively involved in training his children. Mentoring is taking the lead and participating in a young life to teach and train.

Mentoring is a hot topic in business literature today. You can read many books about finding someone to coach your career. Those books have a great point, but the need for an effective mentor is not just for business people. Every boy and girl needs a mentor to help him or her succeed in life.

The word "mentor" comes to us from the Greek epics of Homer. When Odysseus was preparing to leave home to fight in the Trojan War, he asked his most-trusted and wisest counselor, Mentor, to guide the education and training of his son, Telemachus, in his absence. He knew the need for someone wise and experienced to shape and mold a young life.

Notice that Ephesians 6:4 says to *"bring them up in the nurture and admonition of the Lord."* Parents, and primarily the father, are to give children a thorough and effective grounding in the Word of God.

"Hear, O my son, and receive my sayings; and the years of thy life shall be many. I have taught in the way of wisdom; I have led thee in right paths" (Proverbs 4:10–11).

To mentor a child is to say, "Take my hand. As we walk together, I'm going to show you some things to avoid. I'm going to show you the direction to go. I'm going to guide you in the right way." Children need mentoring. They need parents to love them enough to take the time to show them how to live.

Sometimes you will see a child struggling with something in his spirit. As a side note, unless you are paying attention, you will not notice anything wrong until it becomes a huge issue. Put your arm around your child and tell him you love him. Children need reassurance that your love for them will never change. Dr. John

Goetsch, in his book entitled *Mentoring and Modeling,* says, "The very minimum we should do as mentors for those following us, is to guarantee, that we are there for them, that we will unconditionally accept and love them."[14]

Maybe you need to teach how to do simple chores. I have found that children do not know how to sweep. They just push the broom around. It looks worse *after* they "sweep" than it did *before.* You have to show them how to accomplish the task successfully. In every area of life—attitudes, work, finances, walking with God— children need mentors.

We Mentor Children by Nurturing Them

To nurture means "to provide conditions favorable to healthy growth." A gardener who wants healthy crops pulls out the weeds and puts in fertilizer for his plants. In our children's lives, we have to help remove the sins that keep them from being fruitful. We have to put in the Word of God. God commands us to nurture them to help them to grow.

It is a tragedy if our children grow up physically but do not grow up spiritually. This means we must correct the mistakes and curb the passions that would lead them astray. Mentoring means that we must instruct them in the ways of virtue. It means we must answer their questions and give them advice. It means we must spend time with them.

Children need to be able to learn from their parents. There must be an atmosphere in the home that encourages questions. I have had some dads tell me their children asked them tough questions. I always say, "Be glad they're asking you instead of someone else. Do your best to get them the answer." You can always find somebody who can help you get the answer for them. Do not do anything to discourage them from coming to you.

---

[14] Dr. John Goetsch and Dr. Mark Rasmussen, *Mentoring and Modeling* (California: Revival Books, 2002)

I heard about a father and son who went fishing. After a couple of hours, the boy got bored and began to ask his dad questions. He said, "Dad, how does this boat float?" The dad replied, "I don't rightly know." The boy thought a little more and asked, "How do fish breathe underwater?" The dad said, "I don't know."

After a while the boy asked, "Dad, why is the sky blue?" His dad said, "I don't know that either." The boy said, "Dad, you don't mind me asking all these questions do you?" His father replied, "Of course not. If you don't ask questions, you'll never learn anything!"

We Mentor Children by Spending Time with Them

Effective mentoring requires that we invest time and energy in our children. A Cornell University study found that fathers of preschool children spend on average 37.7 seconds per day in real, meaningful contact with their youngsters. In contrast, those same children watch fifty-four hours of television every week.

In 2003, according to the Nielson TV ratings, the most watched shows among children 2–17 were *The Simpsons* and WWF *Wrestling*. A whole generation of children is growing up without nurturing. They are not hearing stories read to them. Their fathers and mothers are not spending the time necessary to mentor them in God's Truth.

By parking the kids in front of the television, we are fertilizing the weeds instead of pulling them. They watch TV all day, and then when they are seventeen and you are having trouble with them, you go looking for help. I have had people, who have done that, say to me, "Pastor, I just don't know what went wrong." Mentoring must begin at an early age.

"My son, eat thou honey, because it is good; and the honeycomb, which is sweet to thy taste: So shall the knowledge of wisdom be unto thy soul: when thou hast found it, then there shall be a reward, and thy expectation shall not be cut off" (Proverbs 24:13–14).

We Mentor Children by Encouraging Them

Look for opportunities to encourage them. Someone said the best way to encourage children is to "catch them doing something right." Our children will receive plenty of negative influences during their lives. They need positive reinforcement from us when they do things right.

Praise and encouragement are powerful tools. They can shape and motivate children to continue on the right path. It is interesting to me to note how many times God brags on His children in the Bible. Of Abraham, God said, *"For I know him, that he will command his children and his household after him, and they shall keep the way of the Lord..."* (Genesis 18:19).

God spoke to Satan about Job and said, *"...Hast thou considered my servant Job, that there is none like him in the earth, a perfect and an upright man, one that feareth God, and escheweth evil?"* (Job 1:8). And at the baptism of Jesus, God said, *"...This is my beloved Son, in whom I am well pleased"* (Matthew 3:17). God is not stingy with words of praise and encouragement.

There was a national survey done by the Human Development and Family Department at the University of Nebraska-Lincoln. They studied families that showed signs of health. They cataloged the attributes of those families. The number one attribute that marked a strong family was appreciation.

Healthy families were marked by showing approval and giving sincere compliments. The family members tried to make each other feel appreciated and good about themselves. Say, "Thank you." Look for ways to show approval. Look for positive actions that you can encourage.

Maintain Consistent Biblical Teaching

The final key to leaving a godly legacy is to teach the Bible to our children. Ephesians 6:4 says we are to bring up our children in *"the admonition of the Lord."* The word *admonish* means "to warn or to caution against specific faults and encourage about what is right." That is exactly what the Bible will do for us. It will warn and caution us against bad behavior.

"All scripture is given by inspiration of God, and is profitable for doctrine, for reproof, for correction, for instruction in righteousness: That the man of God may be perfect, throughly furnished unto all good works" (2 Timothy 3:16–17).

This passage shows us the power of the Word of God. It is not man's word, philosophies, or opinions. The Scripture is profitable. It works. It produces results. Our children need doctrine. Doctrine simply means teaching or a set of beliefs. Children need values. Some parents say they will let their kids make up their own minds about God and religion when they get older.

God does not tell us to let our children make up their own minds. The Bible says to train them up—intentionally direct their steps—in the way they should go (Proverbs 6:23). Reproof and correction need to be administered to bring their lives into line with the teaching of the Word of God.

So many parents are permissive. Whatever the kid wants to do, they just let him do it. When a child disobeys, he needs correction and instruction. The goal of this kind of training is not to make life easier, it is to prepare the child through the teaching of God's Word to be a mature adult, grounded in faith and ready to be used by God.

Consistently Teach the Bible in the Home

Every home should be a Bible institute. God wants our homes to be places where the Bible is more than a piece of furniture or decoration. The Bible is to be a part of our daily lives. Post Scripture verses on the walls. Make the Bible real to your family and follow its instruction.

"Hear, O Israel: The Lord our God is one Lord: And thou shalt love the Lord thy God with all thine heart, and with all thy soul, and with all thy might. And these words, which I command thee this day, shall be in thine heart: And thou shalt teach them diligently unto thy children, and shalt talk of them when thou sittest in thine house, and when thou walkest by the way, and when thou liest down, and when thou risest up. And thou shalt bind them for a sign upon thine hand, and they shall be as frontlets between thine eyes. And thou shalt write them upon the posts of thy house, and on thy gates" (Deuteronomy 6:4–9).

Making the Bible real to your children is not a pastoral philosophy; it is the commandment of God. God wants His Word to permeate our homes. He wants our children to see, hear, and learn the Bible in the home.

Proverbs 1:8 says, *"My son, hear the instruction of thy father, and forsake not the law of thy mother."* This verse clearly lays out for us the role of parents as the primary instructors of values to their children. How can we teach our children in the home in such a way that they hear what we are saying?

TEACH THEM DILIGENTLY

The Hebrew word for teach used in Deuteronomy 6:7 means "to sharpen or whet," just as a soldier would prepare his sword for use in battle. In the same way, we need to be paying attention, looking for opportunities to explain and apply the principles of God's Word. We need to be sharp, alert, and ready to teach.

TEACH THEM DAILY

In our daily routine, we need to be talking about God and the Bible to our children. Far too many parents restrict God to Sundays. He is to be a real presence, daily, in everything we do—walking, sitting, resting—all times of our lives are teaching times.

TEACH THEM DIRECTLY

If we are not careful, we may fall victim to the temptation to delegate this task in the busyness of life. Teaching requires presence and commitment. You cannot raise your children via cell phone and e-mail. It takes a personal touch, nurturing, being there—physically, emotionally, and mentally.

Charles Dickens wrote a letter to his son Henry while he was a student away at college. He gave him a number of pieces of fatherly advice, and then he concluded the letter with these words:

> I most strongly and affectionately impress upon you the priceless value of the New Testament, and the study of that book as the one unfailing guide in life. Deeply respecting it, and bowing down before the character of our Saviour, you cannot go very wrong, and will always preserve at heart a true spirit of veneration and humility.
>
> Similarly, I impress upon you the habit of saying a Christian prayer every night and morning. These things have stood by me all through my life, and remember that I tried to render the New Testament intelligible to you and lovable by you when a mere baby. And so God bless you!

Children do not learn everything the first time. Often they do not understand what we are trying to teach them. Start when they are young. There is something powerful about reading the Bible to our children. It lets them know there is a God in Heaven who loves them. Teach them everything children their age can learn about God. Teach them principles from God's Word.

Consistently Teach the Bible in the Church

Parents need to make certain that their entire family, including their children, is actively involved in a sound, Bible preaching and teaching church.

"And let us consider one another to provoke unto love and to good works: Not forsaking the assembling of ourselves together, as the manner of some is; but exhorting one another: and so much the more, as ye see the day approaching" (Hebrews 10:24–25).

It is not easy to be faithful to church. Everything in the world, literally and figuratively, competes for our time and attention. Church is a vital tool in keeping the family heading in the right direction. You cannot afford to allow your children to miss church. What is being taught from the Bible at the church reinforces, in the minds of our children, the lessons they have been hearing from us at home. The two go hand in hand.

By the way, some people get the idea that church is just for kids. Adults need church, too. Some parents drop their kids off at the church and go on their way. That tells young people the things they are about to hear taught are not that important.

I heard about a church in Florida that had been having monthly family events for the community in an effort to reach new people. They were having a problem with parents dropping their kids off, but not coming themselves. To combat the problem, they sent out this announcement: *"The Magic of Lassie,* a film for the whole family, will be shown at 5 PM in the church hall. Free puppies will be given to all children not accompanied by parents!"

Church attendance is a family matter. Many churches are cutting down their schedules because people have lost interest in coming. Your family needs a solid church that will teach the principles and precepts of the Word of God.

Teaching the Word of God at home and in the church gives our children the tools they need to succeed as Christian parents themselves. It ensures that we are leaving a godly legacy to future generations.

Most Christians know that Hudson Taylor was one of the greatest missionaries in history. Many of us have thrilled to the stories of his incredible trust in God and the impact he had on the nation of China, reaching hundreds of thousands with the Gospel. Many people do not know that Hudson Taylor was part of an amazing heritage.

You see, his great-grandfather, James Taylor, never missed a chance to go and hear John Wesley preach—but not because he loved preaching or believed the Gospel. Taylor went to harass Wesley, even on occasion throwing rocks at Wesley while he preached, but the Holy Spirit worked in his life.

Just two days before James Taylor was to be married, he heard Wesley preach from the text, *"As for me and my house, we will serve the Lord"* (Joshua 24:15). Conviction gripped his heart, and at the wedding reception, he announced to a stunned group of family and friends that he had become a Christian.

Taylor prayed that his family would honor God. He prayed for his descendants to follow after him in serving the Lord. His son and his grandson were both godly Christian men. Hudson Taylor was the fourth generation in his family to serve God, but the story does not end there.

Hudson Taylor's son and grandson helped carry on his work until China was closed to the Gospel. The eighth generation of the Taylor family is living today, and they are also actively involved in God's work. What a godly heritage! This is the kind of impact *you* can have on our world and the future of your family if you will model the Christian life, mentor your children, and maintain consistent Bible teaching.

Study Questions

1. What is the greatest gift a father can give his children?

2. Not only do we need to model, we also need to _____.

3. What are three ways of mentoring your children?

4. Where are the two main places the Bible should be taught?

5. Is your husband/wife relationship reflecting Christ and the church?

6.   How many times have you encouraged your wife or children through words today?

7.   List some ways you can make the Scripture more visible in your home.

8.   Will those who come behind you find you faithful?

Memory Verse

Joshua 24:15—"*And if it seem evil unto you to serve the* LORD, *choose you this day whom ye will serve; whether the gods which your fathers served that were on the other side of the flood, or the gods of the Amorites, in whose land ye dwell: but as for me and my house, we will serve the* LORD."

Conclusion

As I write the final words of this book, I am thankful for the impact of God's Word on my life and family. Oh, there have often been times that I should have been more diligent to learn and apply God's Word as a husband and father. Yet, the reality is, that God's Word and His Spirit have made all the difference for us! Last night as I prepared to go to Atlanta to preach, my son Larry, a junior in Bible college, asked if he could take me to the airport. As we drove to LAX, we talked about the Lord and His work. As Larry dropped me off, he gave me a big hug and told me he loved me. That moment to me was well worth the time and energy we have spent investing spiritually in his life.

Building a firm foundation takes place only as we apply one biblical principle at a time to our lives. The process of building the foundation may seem laborious at times, but we must remember, *"Our labor is not in vain in the Lord."*

Bibliography

CHAPTER TWO
1. Women Employed Institute survey of economic data published April 2004 on their website, www.womenemployed.org

CHAPTER FOUR
2. Gary Smalley, *If Only He Knew,* (Grand Rapids, MI: Zondervan Publishing House, 1979)

CHAPTER SIX
3. Karl Zinsmeister, *Marriage Matters* (The American Enterprise: May/June 1996)
4. Daniel Yankelovich, *Foreign Policy After the Election* (Foreign Affairs Magazine: Fall, 1992)
5. J. Kirby Anderson, *Moral Dilemmas* (Baker Book House: 1997)
6. Daniel P. Moynihan, *Toward a Post-Industrial Social Policy* (The Public Interest, Summer 1989)
7. Lee Iacocca with William Novak, *Iacocca* (New York: Bantam Books, 1984, page 289)

CHAPTER SEVEN
8. Tedd Tripp, *Shepherding a Child's Heart* (Wapwallopen, PA: Shepherd Press, 1995)
9. Tom Peters and Nancy Austin, *A Passion for Excellence* (New York: Random House, 1985)

CHAPTER EIGHT
10. Gary Smalley, *The Key to Your Child's Heart,* (Tennessee: W Publishing Group, 1992)

11. Lowell D. Streiker, *Nelson's Big Book of Laughter,* (Tennessee: Thomas Nelson Publishers, 2000)

CHAPTER NINE
12. Ogden Nash, *The Pocket Book of Ogden Nash* (New York: Pocket Books, 1962) "I Do, I Will, I Have," page 21

CHAPTER TEN
13. Dr. Larry Crabb, *Inside Out* (Pennsylvania: NavPress Publishing Group, 1998)

CHAPTER THIRTEEN
14. Dr. John Goetsch and Dr. Mark Rasmussen, *Mentoring and Modeling* (California: Revival Books, 2002)

ABOUT THE AUTHOR

PAUL CHAPPELL is the senior pastor of Lancaster Baptist Church and president of West Coast Baptist College in Lancaster, California. His biblical vision has led the church to become one of the most dynamic Baptist churches in the nation. His preaching is heard on Daily in the Word, a daily radio broadcast heard across America. Pastor Chappell has four children who are married and serving in Christian ministry. He has been married to his wife Terrie for over thirty years.

Connect with Paul Chappell at PaulChappell.com

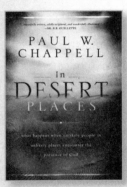
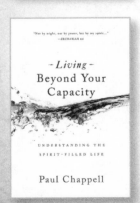

Visit us online

strivingtogether.com

wcbc.edu